They Called Me
Cheesy

Donald M. Edam

Outskirts Press, Inc.
Denver, Colorado

The opinions expressed in this manuscript are solely the opinions of the author and do not represent the opinions or thoughts of the publisher. The author represents and warrants that s/he either owns or has the legal right to publish all material in this book.

They Called Me Cheesy
Tales of growing up in a small Minnesota town in the '30s and '40s

V3.0

Outskirts Press, Inc.
http://www.outskirtspress.com

ISBN: 978-1-4327-1293-8

PRINTED IN THE UNITED STATES OF AMERICA

Preface
In The Beginning

"There is only one success, to be able to spend your life in your own way."

Christopher Morely

It started in first grade, Miss Thor's room, probably in the Fall of 1933. Franklin Delano Roosevelt was well into his first of four terms as President of the United States, which has absolutely nothing to do with this story, but may add a little credibility for those readers who were around at that time. Anyway, our first grade class was studying Holland, with Miss Thor telling us about tulips and dikes and windmills and wooden shoes; about skating on canals and about cheese, Edam Cheese. That's all it took. At recess, I was teased by my classmates, who chased me around the playground shouting: "Edam Cheese! Edam Cheese! Edam Cheese!" Over time, it was shortened to just Cheesy. And the name stuck.

It stuck to the point that even some of my relatives called me by that sobriquet. Much later, in my senior year of high school, someone mentioned "Don Edam" to our

Principal, Miss Vida Mae Lewis who remarked "I didn't know that Cheesy has a brother". She had obviously forgotten about my brother Wendell who had preceded me by ten years, but also shows that Miss Lewis was a solid member of the "Cheesy" faction. Even today, 74 years later, I will sometimes answer the telephone to be greeted by the question: "Is this Cheesy Edam?" which immediately identifies the caller as someone who has roots in Park Rapids, Minnesota.

So, this explains the title that I have selected for this book. And while the book is not an autobiography in the true sense of the word, it is mostly about me, about my childhood and about my adolescent days and about my family with vignettes from some of my later years. It is mostly about my life in the 1930s and 1940s, about some of my memories of those days; halcyon days mostly. Even with the background of the Great Depression and the poverty that accompanied it as well as with the onset of World War II, I still think of those days as 'good days'. It is these 'good days' that I want to tell you about. Why you say? Because, I don't want these good memories to be lost. I want my children, my grandchildren and my great-grandchildren as well as those yet unborn to have a record of some of the facts and experiences that were important to me then. Perhaps these stories will give the reader insights into what life was like back then; why I am as I am, perhaps even why you are as you are.

Writing this book has been therapy for me in ways that I never could have imagined. Searching my memory for juxtaposition of events has caused me to wonder about subjects and happenings that had never occurred to me previously. For example: Who were my ancestors? Where did they come from? Why and how did they come to Minnesota? How did Mom and Grandma Black survive after Dad's death leaving these two women with a total of eight children to care for with absolutely no outside income at that time? Was my sister Elva stillborn or did she die early in her infancy? Where was my dad born? What about his father? Where and when was he born? What of Grandma and Grandpa Sarff? Where did they come from before Indiana? What of Grandpa Canfield? So many questions; and these are only a few that have come to mind since I started to write this. Answers to many of these questions may be gone forever and only give rise to speculation but give me food for thought as I tell these stories. I so wish that I had asked more questions of Mom and Grandma and of Eula and Wen before they passed on.

I must say that searching for these answers has helped to add to information about our family and we may have discovered ancestors and roots from hundreds of years before our first records. We are still looking, although there is good news. Writing this book, raising these and other questions, has led to research that has produced answers to some of the questions posed above. As some of you know, late in 2004 I had a few copies of the book "They Called Me Cheesy" printed for members of the family. Since then, I have discovered some errors and have uncovered some additional facts about our ancestors that need to be included in any family record. Consequently, I have decided to correct and add to that original tome, and re-print it. So those of you who have copies of the first effort, you may discard them or use them to 'scare the mice away' as my mother used to say. The following stories and records are accurate to the best of my ability.

As I have grown older, history has become more meaningful to me, and I hope that it will to my readers as well. After all, how can we know where we're going if we don't know where we've been? Early explorers of the West would frequently look backwards over their shoulders to look at the path that they had just traveled from a different perspective. This was so that they could more readily recognize the trail to be traveled on their return trip. It is not that much different today. Learning of our past can help to prepare us for our future.

Life in these United States has changed so much during my lifetime that I would like my progeny to have a feeling about what small town life was like when I was growing up in northern Minnesota. This is the main reason for telling these stories. I hope that you will be entertained by some of them, that you might learn something of the culture of those decades, and maybe even a little of the history of those times.

Finally, although it may be boring, I would like the readers in my family to know a little about our ancestors. To that end, I have included a discussion of ancestors and genealogy in Chapter XII. This is an ongoing effort. There are copies of some old photographs included. I hope that they will help to add a sense of realism to some of the people and events that are included herein. Maybe you will recognize some of your own features and those of your children that are similar to those belonging to people in these old pictures.

If I mischaracterize certain events, if some of my dates are inaccurate or if I include the wrong people in some of these adventures, I plead guilty now. The following is as I remember it. And only embellished a little bit from time to time. So be it.

My apologies to you teachers amongst my readers; the following is written much as I speak: with complete disregard for the English language and the rules of composition and of punctuation..

So read on, dear reader; although it probably will not be

possible, I would like to discuss this poor effort with each and every one of you. As you all may know already, I love to tell stories, especially about the 'good old days'. Hopefully these stories will all fall into the category of 'history' and not into 'historical fiction'.

This book is dedicated to my family of readers and especially to Claudia who encouraged me to undertake this labor of love. Special thanks to Cathy Edam and to Karen and Paul Packard for their editing and to Claudia for her help, advice, and organization of the photo section, and to Shirley and Morris Edam, my newly found Montana cousins for information about my Grandfather Edam and for his picture. Ruby Sartain furnished old family photos that I didn't know existed. Thank you Cousin Ruby. And finally, thanks to Chris Anderson for scanning and enhancing the photos for this book.

Where To Find It

Chapter I

First Grade Redux

"...if you follow a path that interests you, not to the exclusion of love, sensitivity, and cooperation with others, but with the strength of conviction that you can move others by your own efforts , and do not make success or failure the criteria by which you live, the chances are you'll be a person worthy of your own self respect."

Anonymous

First Grade was very nearly my undoing. I started strong; I was the best reader in the class and Miss Thor would sometimes send me to the Second Grade Room to stand at the front of the room and to read something to them, to show off my reading skills. I had it made. But sadly, things went down hill rapidly from there. Towit:

The boys' washroom was something of an antiquity, although it certainly was a step up from the outdoor two-holer biffy that I was accustomed to at home. No urinals in the boys washroom, just a long continuous wall with a drain at the bottom, much like the ones in use at the USAFA Football Stadium today. Who says we weren't forward looking in Park Rapids back then? But I digress.

During potty breaks, the boy's washroom was frequently crowded, elbow-to-elbow so to speak. One such day I was standing next to a boy that I'd never met even though I think that he was from my room. Even in those early days, I was an outgoing young man, anxious to make new friends, but given to act on impulse. My neighbor's foot was close to mine and very much within my line of fire. The devil made me do it, I think, but with very little additional effort I directed my stream over into his space. For you folks in Rio Linda: I peed on his shoe. He reacted with uncharacteristic lack of cool, and in tears reported me to Miss Thor. When confronted by Miss Thor, I readily confessed, and although reprimanded, I was not punished. But I lost considerable brownie points with my then beloved teacher and mentor.

Unfortunately, I was not finished burning bridges. We are now a few weeks before Thanksgiving, and Miss Thor's first graders are preparing a little Thanksgiving Show complete with songs and pilgrim hats and collars and with paper feathers pinned to our little turkey butts. Miss Thor had neglected to tell us the real reason for all of this preparation or perhaps it was that we were so good that it was decided on the spur of the moment to take our show on the road. Anyway, one cold but sunny morning a few days later as we first graders gathered outside the school waiting for the bell to ring, I was informed by one of my fellow turkeys that "…today we are going to put on our Thanksgiving Show for the second graders."

"Not me!" says I; and as the bell sounded and my friends headed for class, I headed for home. I hadn't signed up to do shows in front of the second graders and wasn't about to comply. Indeed, where was this going to end? The third graders would probably be next, and after that who knows?

As I wended my way home, reality finally began to set in. I was pretty sure (my first rational thought of the day) that my mother was not going to share my enthusiasm for my one-person boycott. She no doubt would not understand my extreme reluctance to parade in front of the second graders shamelessly shaking my paper-feather covered booty. So I lingered on my way home, stopping at one of the old warehouses not far from home to meditate on the fate that was soon to befall me. Nor was I wrong. To say that Mom was disappointed in me would be an understatement. But she didn't punish me. Rather she announced that she and I were going to visit Miss Thor after lunch. Corporal punishment administered then and there would have been my choice, had it been offered. But alas, it was not.

So that afternoon, the three of us met privately. Mom cried. Miss Thor cried. And yes, I wept also. But the worst was yet to come.

A few weeks later, our room was preparing for our Christmas Party. Miss Thor asked for volunteers to be Santa Claus, to wear a red suit and to pass out Christmas presents to the rest of the class. I, of course, enthusiastically raised my hand, to which Miss Thor responded, "No, not you Don, you can't be trusted". Although an accurate statement, and seemingly of little consequence at the time, I carried the burden of these words for the remainder of my time in first grade and well into succeeding grades. Indeed, I still flush with embarrassment and regret from the sting of those long forgotten (by others) words in front of my classmates. Who says children don't have long memories? I will always remember. I will never forget! Thus did my young and fragile psyche suffer its first of many dents.

Chapter II

Where and How We Lived

"Nothing that can happen to you is half so important as the way in which you meet it...Nobody can be sure when disaster, disappointment, injustice or humiliation may come to him through no fault of his own. Nor can one be guaranteed against one's own mistakes and failures. But the way we meet life is ours to choose and when integrity, fortitude, dignity and compassion are our choice, the things that can happen to us lose their power over us."

Ina Corinne Brown

We moved a lot when I was little and kept right on moving until I had finished college and still some more after that. As near as I can remember and during my life so far, I have lived in 28 different houses or apartments in 13 different cities or towns and in 9 different states, not counting the ship and bases where I served when

I was in the Navy. But the place that I think of most is the neighborhood where I was born and the houses in that neighborhood on the south edge of Park Rapids, Minnesota. This is where we lived until I started junior high school.

Dad worked for the Great Northern Railroad in Long Prairie, Minnesota and moved to Park Rapids shortly before I was born. We have never owned a home in Park Rapids but rented various houses in the same neighborhood starting with the house where I was born. Shortly thereafter, we moved to a nicer house on the west side of the railroad tracks that we called Crowley's House. We lived there until Dad drowned while duck hunting in 1930; then back across the tracks to houses that were next door and/or across the street from my birthplace.

What a shock Dad's death must have been to Mom. While we were far from wealthy, we were certainly not living in poverty. Dad had a good job at the Great Northern; we owned a car and a piano, and Wen had a pony. Our future must have appeared to have been assured and at least comfortable. All of that changed overnight, literally. Suddenly Mom was left with three kids ages two (me) ten (Wen) and seventeen (Eula). We had no insurance, no income and very few assets. In addition, Mom and Grandma Black had combined to look after my five cousins who were essentially orphaned when their mother (Mom's sister Ella) died in 1928 and their father took off only to return on rare occasions and, as far as I know, contributed little if anything to the family welfare.

After Dad's death, we moved to an awful house across the street from where I was born. Thankfully, we only stayed there a few months and then moved back across the street to what I have always called the Gray House. It was a small frame house with weathered siding, hence the gray color. It was a decent house by the living standards of those days although I expect that many of my readers would not know how to deal with some of the aspects of our daily lives. This is where we lived until Mom's untimely death in 1939.

The Gray House was not far from the south edge of town, close to the stockyards, east of the Great Northern Railroad tracks, and only a few hundred yards from the Fish Hook River below the Minnesota Power & Light dam. It was a two-story, three-bedroom house with a small living room, a rather large dining room, a kitchen, a root cellar, a woodshed and a small barn with a hay loft. Those were the good features. It had no, and I mean NO insulation. It also had no electricity and no indoor plumbing. The house is still there at 319 6th Street East, the second house west of Riverside Avenue, but its appearance has changed considerably since we lived there. The first house east of the Gray House is the house where I was born.

The house was heated (and I use the term loosely) by a wood burning stove in the living room supplemented by a wood burning range in the kitchen. In the winter, we closed up the kitchen during those cold months and moved the kitchen stove into the dining room which helped to keep the rest of the house a little warmer.

The living room stove would qualify as a 'pot-bellied stove'. It occasionally would have red hot areas on its sides when the fire was burning well and one could burn oneself seriously unless care was exercised. A stovepipe about six inches in diameter extended upward from the stove into the ceiling and into the bedroom above.

If we still had the kitchen range today, it would be a classic antique. Split wood was fed into the stove through removable lids on its surface. A large oven took up most of the space on the bottom portion of the range and there were two warming ovens that extended across the top and a reservoir on the right side that held water that was warmed by the cooking fire. Mom sometimes kept a few cast iron irons on the surface for use in ironing clothes and also to warm our beds on cold winter nights.

Fuel for the two stoves varied depending upon the price and availability of wood, but mostly we burned slabs. Slabs were the leftover trimmings from logs that were being sawed into lumber at the sawmill. Slabs had no commercial value except for fuel. They didn't produce as much heat as more expensive fuels but they were cheap which was why we burned them. Occasionally, we would buy a truck load of tamarack or poplar. The latter was called 'popple' and burned a little better than slabs. Many of my friends lived in homes heated by coal burning furnaces (the best) or burned hardwoods such as birch, next best. The living room was generally warm enough, except in the morning when the fire had burned down or even gone out completely. The dining room was also warm enough especially after we had moved the kitchen stove into the dining room for the winter.

Eula's room, above the living room, was the warmest of the bedrooms, because the stove pipe from the living room stove passed through her room. Wen's room was next to the living room on the same floor, and although it was on the north side of the house received some of the benefit from the living room stove. I slept in the same bed with Mom until I was six or seven years old, when I moved in with Wen. Mom's and my room was on the second floor on the north side of the house; the coldest room in the house. We received very little heat from the stove and it was COLD up there. Where was 'global warming' when we needed it? On really cold nights, and we had lots of those, Mom let me sleep in Dad's fleece lined overcoat. She would also take the chill off the bed by putting irons that had been heated on the kitchen stove and wrapped in newspapers between the sheets at the foot of the bed. If one didn't burn one's feet on the hot irons it was possible to stay relatively warm. I, of course, was snug in Dad's coat. But how Mom stayed warm, I'll never know. She may have slept in a coat as well, but it couldn't have been as warm as Dad's. We would wake up in the morning with a quarter of an inch of frost on the north facing window. We would hurry down to the living room, restart the fire, and dress in front of the stove, warm on the near-side (taking care not to burn one's backside on the hot stove) and freezing on the far-side.

There were no carpets or rugs in the house. Floors were made of wide, probably ten inch, pine planks worn smooth by traffic over the years. Furniture was simple: a round drop leaf table with matching well used chairs in the kitchen in the summer that would be moved into the dining room in the winter. A tall cupboard stood against the wall in the dining room; it had a decorative panel at the top that would fall off easily. I was struck on the head more than once by this panel if I got a little rambunctious and bumped into this dangerous piece of furniture. A rocking chair and a small davenport with our Baldwin upright piano, all in the living room, completed the décor of the Gray House.

Each autumn, as the days grew shorter and colder, Mom and Wen took some unique actions to make the house a little warmer. They would buy a few rolls of heavy building paper and nail the paper all around the outside base of the house using lath to keep the paper in place. Wen would then heap shovels full of dirt all around the house where the building paper met the ground. We called this 'banking the house' and it effectively sealed the base of the house against the winds and weather and kept the house a little warmer. Wen also covered the outside of all of the windows with translucent oil cloth. Although we couldn't see through it, the cloth let in some light and served as inexpensive storm windows. It remained in place until spring.

Our toilet was a two-holer out by the barn complete with Montgomery Ward catalogs for reading etc (mostly etc). In the summer Mom planted morning glories that grew on a lattice that shielded the door and gave the whole affair a fragrant air (no pun intended). Going to the toilet was sometimes somewhat of a social event, especially if we had company and the weather was good. Young people frequently went in gender matched pairs. Winter visits were kept to a bare minimum (pun intended) because one risked serious damage to the tender parts of ones anatomy if one lingered too long.

Outside the kitchen/wood shed door was our water supply; a cast iron hand pump that required priming and patience and care each time it was used. During the winter months there was always a sloped accumulation of ice around the base of the pump requiring great care to avoid slipping and falling while pumping. Priming the pump in the winter was somewhat of an art, because warm water had to be used to thaw the pump, yet using hot water was risky because it might cause the frigid cast iron to crack. The well was not deep, but the water was good. And in the summer we lowered milk and butter and other perishables in buckets into the well in order to keep the contents cool.

Later on we acquired an icebox for the kitchen. It was a large wooden affair with a number of doors; one for holding a small block of ice, and others for storing food. A special memory of that icebox is of a large crock of milk covered with cream so thick that you could skim it off with a spoon. Yum! In the summer, every few days or so, ice would be delivered to our door by the iceman who drove a horse drawn flatbed wagon. For the kids in the neighborhood, this was an event! We would run after the wagon and collect ice chips that the iceman created as he trimmed a block to fit the compartment in the icebox. Then using a large pair of tongs he would sling the block unto his shoulder, protected by a short leather cape and carry it into the kitchen. Sometimes we carried a shaker of salt with us to sprinkle onto the ice. Why? It seemed to be the thing to do and it tasted good.

We generally kept a milk cow in the barn, a flock of various kinds of chickens in a fenced pen and occasionally a pig who lived in the pen with the chickens. The chicken flock was replenished each spring by mail order. It was quite an occasion when the loudly peeping new chicks arrived at the post office in their flat ventilated cardboard boxes. Surprisingly, most arrived alive. Then we had to arrange for a heated area in the woodshed until they were able to survive out of doors.

Mom sold milk and eggs to the neighbors and sometimes sold chickens to Roessler's Butcher Shop on Main Street. Until Eula started teaching at a rural school and Wen started bringing in some of his part time job earnings, these animals were our sole source of income. I helped collect eggs and even milked the cow sometimes. I also got to help Wen slaughter the chickens. I didn't mind helping to chop their heads off because that was kind of fun; headless chickens would run around the yard for a few seconds until their life force dwindled. Plucking the feathers was OK also. But sometimes the butcher wanted the chickens delivered with their heads in place, which meant that we had to slit their throats. I didn't care for that much. We also had a neighbor who was out of work who used to help himself to our chickens once in awhile. He had a large family to feed, so Mom never complained. She probably would have given them to him had he asked.

On infrequent occasions when we butchered a pig, our cousins would come over and help Wen to butcher the creature. It was an all day event, almost like a party and we always looked forward to it. Wen would shoot the pig with his .22 rifle, cut its throat, hang it up and gut it, and then scald it so that the bristles could be scraped off. After that the carcass was hung up in the woodshed where it was cut up and packaged for eating. Butchering was generally done in the late fall so that the meat would be frozen solidly in the winter, and would generally have to be cut up with a meat saw.

In the summer, Mom planted a large garden mostly for vegetables but with some flowers as well. Each spring, Mom would hire Mr. Nagle to prepare the garden for planting. He would arrive with his team of horses, a horse drawn plow and a drag. Within a few hours, the garden would be ready for planting. It was a treat to follow Mr. Nagle, he with the reins slung over his shoulders, speaking to the horses in his own mono-syllables, guiding the plow in neat parallel rows. The rich black earth rolled off the plow in moist sweet smelling curls. When finished with the plow, he would hitch the horses to the drag, and standing on it would retrace his route again and again until the soil was loose and flat and ready for planting.

Mom grew tomatoes, potatoes, sweet corn, carrots, radishes, cabbage, onions, cucumbers and dill for pickles in the fall. Flowers were generally pansies, cosmos and petunias with a few sunflowers. Sometimes we ate dandelion greens from the yard. They tasted a lot like spinach which I didn't like much either.

In spite of our lack of cash, we ate pretty well, all things considered. I have mentioned the crock of milk in the icebox with cream to be skimmed for cereal but also to be churned into butter. We had a small hand-turned churn for butter making. It was fun to turn at first, but soon became a chore as the mixture became thick and heavy. But when it was finished there was a large blob of butter swimming in buttermilk. The butter was salted and together with a glass of cold buttermilk and freshly baked warm bread made quite a feast.

Mom taught me how to make and bake cake, from scratch yet. And there were eggs and bacon and side pork and vegetables and sometimes chicken for Sunday dinner. ('Dinner' was at noon and 'supper' was in the early evening. We didn't have 'lunch' until much later in life when 'lunch' moved into 'dinnertime' and 'dinner' took over for 'supper' which disappeared forever. Thankfully, 'breakfast' remained where it always had been.) On one such Sunday dinner, we were eating at the kitchen table, as usual, and as I munched on a tasty drumstick, I looked out of the window for my pet rooster, Buff, a large orange creature that was my favorite. Not seeing him I asked, "Where's ol' Buff?" The following silence at the table told me that Buff and I were much closer at that moment than I wanted to be.

Spring was 'sucker' spearing time. Each spring, schools of rough fish called 'suckers' together with their cousins called 'redhorse' both close relatives of carp, would appear in the Fish Hook River to spawn below the dam. Wen and our cousins Bill and Ken would get out the spears, long handled multi-tined creations and go fishing below the Red Bridge. They would return a few hours later, soaking wet, carrying gunny sacks full of these fish, each in the two to four pound range. Then would begin a fish cleaning frenzy. The fish were quite oily so were best when smoked. But the roe (fish eggs that is) would be cooked up immediately and were quite tasty. When the municipal sewer system came to

Park Rapids with the sewage treatment plant installed between the dam and the Red Bridge, with treated effluent flowing into the Fish Hook River there, sucker spearing understandably came to an end.

In the summer we fished for sunfish and bluegills and the occasional pike in the millpond below the dam. They were delicious and fun to catch.

Wen was a hunter and contributed pheasants and ducks to the table during their respective seasons and rabbits and squirrels year round. I was frequently drafted into holding the rabbit and squirrel carcasses while Wen skinned and cleaned them. I didn't like that much, and on one occasion complained tearfully, "What did they ever do to you?"

I didn't mind helping to clean and pluck the ducks and pheasants. This was probably due to my vast chicken plucking experience. We had to be very careful with the rabbits because they were sometimes diseased and had lesions under their skins and could not be eaten. I think that tularemia was the disease that we were concerned about.

We always had guns around the house. Dad had a Western Field 12 gauge pump shotgun.

I even had a small .22 Savage single action rifle for awhile when I was eleven or twelve years old. And, at that time, Wen had an old 12 gauge single shot shotgun that broke down into three pieces. He kept it broken down at the foot of the stairs in the Gray House. One fall afternoon, Wen came running into the house shouting, "They're coming, they're coming! Get the gun, get the gun!" He had just sighted a flock of geese flying very low and their course was going to take them directly over our house. By the time Wen had fumbled with the three pieces of his shotgun and finally had it assembled and loaded, the geese were long gone and Wen was livid.

Another disadvantage of the Gray House was that we

had rats that lived in the woodshed and probably under the house as well. My only encounter was on one dark summer evening, when I was playing in the back yard and a rat tried to run up my pants leg, but thankfully couldn't get past my knee. It scared the daylights out of me but there was no harm done. That event probably stimulated Wen to do a little rat extermination. Wen took his shotgun into the woodshed one evening and set up a stake out. Later, while we were having supper in the kitchen, suddenly a very loud explosion was heard from the woodshed. Wen had dispatched one of the creatures. He must have poisoned the rest because I don't recall any more problems.

During Wen's last couple of years in high school, Wallace Ericsson, a friend of his that lived on a farm about 15 miles southeast of town became our boarder during the winter when rural roads were frequently snowed shut. Mr. and Mrs. Ericsson, a happy, round, red-faced Scandinavian couple, would bring Wallace to our house on Sunday evenings and would pick him up on Friday afternoons, weather permitting. They paid for his room and board with food from their farm. We looked forward to Sunday evenings to see what bounty the Ericssons had brought for the coming week. The bags and boxes contained such wonders as slabs of bacon, hams, roasts, liver, chickens, eggs, butter, cream, milk, home-baked bread etc. Not all of this every week, mind you, but enough to make this an event to be anticipated.

We had other boarders from time-to-time when we lived in the Gray House. There were two brothers, Sid and Len Pitney who were amateur boxers. They installed a punching bag and some other basic training equipment in the barn and even made a punching bag for me out of a gunny sack stuffed with corn husks. Eula had a crush on Sid who was pretty good looking as I remember. Nothing came of it, I think, but maybe I was just too young to recognize the signs.

There was another boarder, Dean Hedlund, who with Wen, played trumpet in the Night Owls, a dance band that practiced in our living room frequently. More about that later. Dean taught me how to build model airplanes from kits of balsa wood and tissue paper. The first effort was a Curtis Robin, a high wing monoplane, and the second effort was a duplicate, only this time, I did it all by myself. After that I lost count of all the models that I built; some turned out nicely, some not so great. Some actually flew for short distances.

One other boarder that I remember was Gene Brietbach who played baritone horn in the high school band. He would serenade us after supper sometimes. Years later, I played that very same horn in the high school band after the only horn player graduated and I was promoted(?) from trumpet player to this instrument that I grew to love, eventually, sort of.

The complete lack of insulation in the house that caused the house to be so cold in the winter had the opposite effect in the summer; it let the heat in during the day and kept it hot inside well into the night. I can remember a few hot summer nights when Mom would let me sleep on the floor in front of the screen door to the porch. Sometimes a weak breeze would find its way into the room, but mostly I would lie there, sweltering, listening to the mosquitoes humming on the screens.

And with the heat came thunder storms. 1936 was a record year for cold and a record year for heat, and thunder storms. When it would storm, and it seems as though it was generally at night, Mom would get us all out of our beds and we would wait out the storm sitting together in the kitchen. She hated storms and especially lightning and I guess that she figured that if we were going to die, we might as well all go together. One such night, we were all gathered together in the kitchen with the wind howling, rain pelting the window, lightning flashing and thunder crashing. As I recall, one moment I was sitting on the kitchen table engaged in the groups conversation, and the next moment I found myself sitting in the middle of the kitchen floor with a lingering vision of a blinding flash of light and with no memory of any sound. Lightning had struck and destroyed a pine tree at the corner of the woodshed about 20 feet from where we were sitting. The tree provided one of the supports for my swing, now gone. Thankfully, there was no damage to the house.

During this same storm, winds tore the roof off of one of the warehouses about 100 yards from our house and also removed the roof from the grandstand at the fairgrounds on the other side of town.

Severe storms were not limited to summers in Northern Minnesota. One of the worst blizzards in Minnesota history swept in from the Dakotas on November 11, 1941; hence its name 'The Armistice Day Blizzard'. (For you American history deprived readers, World War I ended on November 11, 1918 with the signing of an armistice. This date was called Armistice Day and was celebrated as a national holiday for many years. Today, it is known as Veteran's Day and scarcely recognized.) Anyway, with the absence of reliable weather forecasting in those years, this fast moving storm caught most North Dakota and Minnesota residents off-guard resulting in death to many cattle and to some people. Blinding snow driven by blizzard force winds blanketed Park Rapids with deep snow packed drifts. The first floors of the stores and businesses on the west side of main street were completely covered by drifts. The next day, store owners had to dig tunnels through these drifts in order to get into their stores. This was an exercise in futility because, except for us kids, there were not many people on Main Street that day. But we kids had a ball! Skiing was great. We found our way out to the County Fair Grounds and spent hours jumping off of the roofs of the fair buildings into the deep drifts below. And schools were closed for two glorious days.

One of the stories that came out of this storm that demonstrates the danger and the ferocity of a Minnesota blizzard tells of an incident that occurred on Highway 10 west of Detroit Lakes. A couple in an automobile were stalled a few feet behind a school bus, also stalled by drifts on the highway and nearly zero visibility. The man in the car told his wife that he was going to go up to the school bus to see how the kids were doing. He never made it. Confused by the storm, his frozen body was found days later about a half-mile from his car.

Some farmers, harking back to the dust bowl days of the mid-30's, were able to rig ropes between the house and the barn in winter so that they could get safely back and forth to care for their animals.

Unless you have spent a few minutes outside in such a blizzard, it is difficult to appreciate and understand the disorientation that comes from the sting of snow and ice particles being driven into your face and eyes and being buffeted by gale force winds. The wind literally takes your breath away and leaves you gasping for air. You readers who have spent winters in North Dakota and northern Minnesota will understand.

Wen was goose hunting south of town that day when the blizzard struck in mid-afternoon, and was fortunate to make it safely back home. Some did not.

Allow me to regale you with another cold weather story. One winter weekend, Wen asked me if I wanted to go ice fishing with him. I agreed since it would be a new experience for me. Wen drove an old '35 or '36 Chevy four-door back then. He couldn't afford to buy anti-freeze so he just used water in the radiator. This meant that he had to drain the radiator after every time that he drove it in cold weather in order to keep the fluid from freezing and cracking the engine block. So, that day, he filled the radiator with water, got the car started and we drove to a small lake southeast of town. Wen drove out onto the snow covered ice, stopped the car and drained the radiator since the temperature was well below freezing. He built a small windbreak out of snow blocks to shield a small fire, chopped two holes in the ice and we proceeded to fish. I don't remember what we were using for bait, but it made no difference because we caught nothing. As the sun approached the horizon and the day became even colder, we decided to start for home. So, Wen dipped water out of the holes in the ice and refilled the radiator. But, the car wouldn't start! The cold had congealed the oil in the crankcase and the cylinders until the engine was so stiff that it wouldn't turn over. At that moment the prospects for the rapidly approaching night did not seem at all promising. We were miles from the closest shelter and it was getting dark and very cold.

What Wen did next has continued to amaze me over the years. We collected sticks and small pieces of wood from the shoreline and soaking it with gasoline siphoned from the gas tank, Wen started a small fire directly under the crankcase. In due time, the engine was warmed to the point that he was able to get it started. We drove home in a cold car that seemed warm by comparison and arrived home cold but safe. But what if the car had not started? What if we had been forced to spend the night in the car or had decided to try to hike to safety in below zero temperatures?

What if Wen's little warming fire had started the engine on fire before he could get it started? I've relived that afternoon many times over the years and have concluded that Someone was looking after us that day; even though we didn't catch any fish.

Did I mention that the Gray House didn't have any electricity when we moved in? Many of the houses in the neighborhood did not have electricity then so we did not feel particularly deprived. We used kerosene lamps for light, the kind with large, glass chimneys and wicks that extended down into the fuel. They required quite a bit of attention; the chimneys had to be cleaned, the wicks trimmed and the lamps filled with kerosene. The chimneys were quite fragile and broke frequently, especially if I got a little rambunctious with my wooden sword. We had a kerosene lantern for trips to the barn and to the biffy after dark.

One spring day I came home from school to find Victor Levinick, who ran the Ben Franklin Store as a primary occupation, hard at work wiring our house. So suddenly we had electric lights! Not long after that we acquired an old, used Atwater-Kent radio in a carved wooden cabinet about three feet tall. It was wonderful!

After school I would hurry home to listen to my favorite programs: The Lone Ranger ("Hi ho Silver…away!"), Captain Midnight ("Bong, bong, bong…"), Jack Armstrong, The All-American Boy ("Have you tried Wheaties…"), Tom Mix and many others, but these were my favorites. We would listen to WDAY Fargo with the Texas Ranger and his cohorts; to WNAX Yankton and the Gurney family selling Chinese Elm windbreaks; and to WCCO Minneapolis.

Saturday afternoons in the fall I would tune into the University of Minnesota Golden Gopher's football games.

And what games they were! Minnesota had two National Championships in the mid-'30s under Coach Bernie Bierman. The good games were always with Michigan for the Little Brown Jug, with Wisconsin, Purdue and other teams in the Big Ten. We sometimes played Nebraska and sometimes Nebraska even scored. When we played Iowa I was able to listen to the game on WHO Des Moines and the announcer would be Ronnie "Dutch" Reagan, the same man who later occupied the White House for two history making Republican terms. (The Democrats are still having a cow about those eight years in the '80s and are still trying to re-write that history).

I still remember many of the players on those teams; Ed Widseth, Bud Wilkinson, Horace Bell and Julie Alphonse. I was heart broken when Andy Uram broke his wrist against Wisconsin the week before the Notre Dame game which we lost 7 – 6 without Andy. It was during those years when the 'Galloping Gophers' a traveling basketball team made up of football players came to town to play an exhibition game with the local Company L Team. There they were in person! My football heroes! What a thrill!

With the advent of electricity in our home, Mom was able to buy a well used washing machine that we kept in the woodshed. It had a corrugated copper tub with a roller wringer mounted above it. Using water heated on the kitchen stove Mom would wash clothes once a week. She would let me help her wring water from the clothes taking them from the machine and passing them through the wringer into a tub filled with cold rinse water. They would then be hung from clothes lines out in the yard using wooden clothes pins. Clothes taken from the outdoor lines always smelled so fresh that the aroma was almost intoxicating. In the winter, clothes would freeze stiff, so that many times they were hung inside from a wooden clothes rack. Before the arrival of the washing machine, Mom did washing by hand, putting soiled clothes in a boiler filled with hot water on the stove. Imagine how much work that involved!

In the same vein, our periodic baths were conducted in a galvanized tub filled with heated water in the kitchen. Serious contortions were required by the bather to participate in this operation. It wasn't until I started playing basketball in junior high that I had my first shower. As I recall, some of my junior high school teachers complained, understandably, about the aroma that arose from the many unwashed bodies in their classrooms during the winter months when cold weather discouraged baths and bathing and elevated temperatures in the classroom accentuated the presence of these vapors. And, teachers did not make a lot of money then either.

Summer was my favorite season in the Gray House. My friends all lived close by: Don, Helen and Chuckie Town were next door; and Chuckie Wilkins next door the other way. Sonny Myers lived just across the tracks, and most summers, Leo John Sloan came to visit his aunt who lived close by. My cousin Leo lived not too far away and sometimes some of my classmates came over. I rarely had no one to play with.

One episode of note found Chuckie Town and I climbing in a group of elm trees that had been planted along a boulevard close to their house. The mature trees had grown so that their branches were interlaced. If one were careful, one could climb from tree-to-tree for the entire length of the boulevard. The trees were well leafed out this particular day so although Mrs. Town could see me, Chuckie was obscured from her view. Standing below one of the trees, the very one that Chuckie occupied at the moment, Mrs Town called to me and asked if Chuckie was up there. I assured her that he was not; but, unfortunately Chuckie picked that instant to lose his grip and came hurtling through the branches landing at his mother's feet. Chuckie, unhurt, went home in tears, and I, wisely, remained in the trees until the coast was clear.

Another episode, one in which I was not involved thankfully, featured the other Chuckie. He and some other kids were playing in the hayloft of their barn. At one point in time, Chuckie came running into their kitchen asking his grandma for a glass of water. Clutching the glass of water he streaked out of the house only to return moments later with a similar request. On his third such return, Grandma Wilkins suspecting something untoward, followed him outside to find that he and his friends had been playing with matches and had set the barn on fire. A quick call to the local volunteer fire department and the arrival of one of their two trucks soon had the fire under control, no harm done. I don't think that they called it 'grounding' in those days.

But the evenings were the best. We played in the street in front of our house and we called it 'playing under the arc light'. I don't know where this term came from although there was a street light at the end of the street, which did give us some light to play in. Our street was unpaved, and we played games such as pomp-pomp-pullaway, hide-and-seek, tincan-knockoff, star-light-star-bright to name a few. And they were fun. The 'big kids'generally came to play with us 'little kids' and that was the most fun. The 'big kids' were 12 to 16 years old and they entered our games as semi-equals. Sometimes after it got too dark to play anymore, the 'big kids' left to play their 'own games' and we had to go inside.

Our celebration of Halloween in those days was much different than it is today. We didn't go trick or treating.

Instead, we rang doorbells and ran away. We put trash on doorsteps. We soaped windows until Mom told me that we shouldn't do that especially to the older people's homes. The big kids sometimes tipped over outdoor toilets which led to many funny stories, to us, especially about those structures that happened to be occupied at the time of the tipping.

Have you ever heard of a 'shivaree' or more correctly a "charivari"? This was a fun custom that was still practiced in the mid '30s. Marriages were frequently conducted at the home of one of the participants, generally the bride. After that ceremony, generally in the early evening, friends and neighbors of the newly wedded couple would gather outside the home and armed with pans, and kettles, wooden spoons, cow bells and other noise making devices would create a continuous racket until the happy couple would present themselves to the crowd and favor them with a long and lingering kiss. Sometimes refreshments were served, but the noise making was the most fun. This is another bit of fun that seems to have disappeared over the years.

Mom died suddenly in late summer, 1939 and my halcyon childhood days came to an end.

Wen and Eula and I left the Gray House and moved in with our cousins and with Grandma Black for a month or so. We were very crowded and we cousins didn't get along that well in such close quarters. So we three remaining Edams moved into an apartment that was half of a house kitty-cornered from the house where I was born. It had electricity but no indoor plumbing. It was heated by an oil fueled stove in the living room, and for the first time that I could remember, we were warm in the winter. Mrs. Dutton, the owner, who lived in the other half of the house, had a telephone! So we could sometimes ask her if we could use the phone and she always graciously complied. No pushbuttons or dials; just ask the operator to connect you with a three digit number, or, if you didn't know the number, just ask her to connect you with so-and-so. No problem.

Just before the United States entered World War II a universal draft system was introduced. Wen failed his physical because of an undersized heart, and was declared 4-F so he didn't have to go. Shortly thereafter, Wen married Bonnie Jean Swaim, a pretty and very nice young lady who lived on Fish Hook Lake and who he had been courting for some time. With Wen no longer there, Eula and I moved into a small apartment above the Gamble Hardware Store on Main Street. As my older cousins went to war, Grandma Black and the remaining cousins moved into an apartment above the Ben Franklin Store, immediately across Main Street from ours.

Using my bow, I shot an arrow, with a light string attached, across Main Street. Leo and I then strung a copper wire across Main Street between our bedroom windows and with the help of two borrowed amplifiers we had our own private telephone system, until someone complained. Shortly after that Leo joined the Navy.

Eula worked at the Ben Franklin Store then and with Wen's help managed to support the two of us while I attended junior high school and then high school in the new school only a few blocks away. I wasn't home much after that except to eat and to sleep. I became involved in Boy Scouts, then in high school athletics; spent more time with my new friends and at Schmeiders Soda Fountain a few doors up Main Street and in various part time jobs. We ate out a lot then at various restaurants on Main Street because Eula was generally too tired to cook after she got home from work.

One of the few benefits of living on Main Street was that our bedroom window looked out on the street.

Saturday nights in summer were always a spectacle. The population of Park Rapids nearly doubles in the summer, and Saturday was the biggest shopping day of the week. So, Main Street was packed to overflowing on Saturday evenings. The Municipal Liquor Store was directly across the street from our apartment which added to the fun of sitting in our window and watching the people promenade below. My friends would look up and wave and we would have a shouted conversation. The crowd would grow more animated, the music would become louder, and the people-watching would get better until about midnight when Saturday ended and Sunday began and Main Street became quiet once more. I never hear *The Wabash Cannonball* or *San Antonio Rose* without thinking of Main Street on summer Saturday nights.

Wen worked at Green's Grocery before and shortly after he and Bonnie Jeanne were married. Then he moved up Main Street to Bishops Department Store where he managed the shoe department for many years. The spring of my freshman year in high school, Wen got me a part time job (full time in summer) at Bishops where I worked after school and Saturdays until my senior year. During summers when I worked full-time, I worked from 9:00 AM until 9:00 PM in the evening (10:00 PM on Saturdays) six days a week. For this I earned $45.00 per month and received a discount on shoes and clothing. Not much but it helped with groceries and with some of my personal needs. That was the beginning of my working life and except for my time in the Navy and some times in college I have worked for the rest of my life, a total of 65 years so far. And I don't think that I'm done yet.

About twenty miles west of Park Rapids is the Ponsford Indian Reservation, home to many members of the Chippewa Tribe of Native Americans. Many of the young people on the reservation were bused to Park Rapids High School as were our other rural students. Although many attended, very few graduated. At that time, and perhaps now as well, it was illegal to sell alcohol to Indians. To circumvent this law, Indians who were predisposed to consumption of alcohol went to great lengths to obtain their beverage of choice. For example: many automobile owners used pure alcohol in the radiators of their cars because it was cheaper than anti-freeze. There were a number of deaths recorded on the reservation, in those years, from drinking alcohol drained from automobile radiators. Indians would buy and drink hair tonic, mouth wash and other cosmetics containing alcohol. This practice was not limited to the males of the Indian population. One bitterly cold night as I was walking home on Main Street, I heard a child crying as I passed a side street. I could see a child standing by a shape huddled on the snow on the side street not far from where I passed. As I investigated, it became apparent that an Indian child was standing by an Indian woman lying in the snow. Thinking that the poor woman had slipped and fallen and hurt herself, I helped her to her feet. It was soon obvious that she was dead drunk and had been drinking some sweet smelling drink such as hair tonic or perfume. I called the police who took the pair to jail, where they were at least out of the freezing cold.

Park Rapids, or rather Hubbard County, operated a facility known amongst the citizenry as 'the poor house' or 'the old-folks home'. It was a large two-story, frame house with a large porch located on Highway 34 east of town. Regardless of its name, this building was the last stop for those county residents who could no longer care for themselves or who had no one to provide for their care during the last days of their lives. Unfortunate folks who became residents of this facility, seemed to disappear from the Park Rapids scene. One might catch glimpses of them during warm weather in rocking chairs on the front porch of the building. But then they were gone and they ceased to exist. Fortunately, none of my family or anyone that I knew well succumbed to this fate.

This chapter would not be complete if I did not spend a few sentences on Christmases in the Gray House. Christmases that I remember the best were those during our early years in the Gray House. Wen would cut a tree from the nearby forest and it would be set up in the living room. Mom would decorate the tree with strings of popcorn and with tinsel and a few garlands from years past. She would clip small candles onto the tips of tree branches although these candles were rarely lighted because of the danger of setting the tree and hence the house on fire; not an uncommon occurrence in those days. We were poor. Money for gifts competed with money for food and clothing and for rent. Meager gifts were expected and were accepted in kind except for one Christmas that I shall never forget. Even though forewarned that there would not be very many presents under the tree on Christmas Eve, I nevertheless bitterly cried when the packages yielded only a few books for me. I am ashamed about my conduct that year, but I still remember each of the books: *Robin Hood, Billy Whiskers* (which I still have) and a book of the presidents of the United States up through Franklin D. Roosevelt. In subsequent Christmases, I received a sled, a pair of pine skis, and a wind-up train set with a circular track. But the 'book' Christmas is the one that is still remembered.

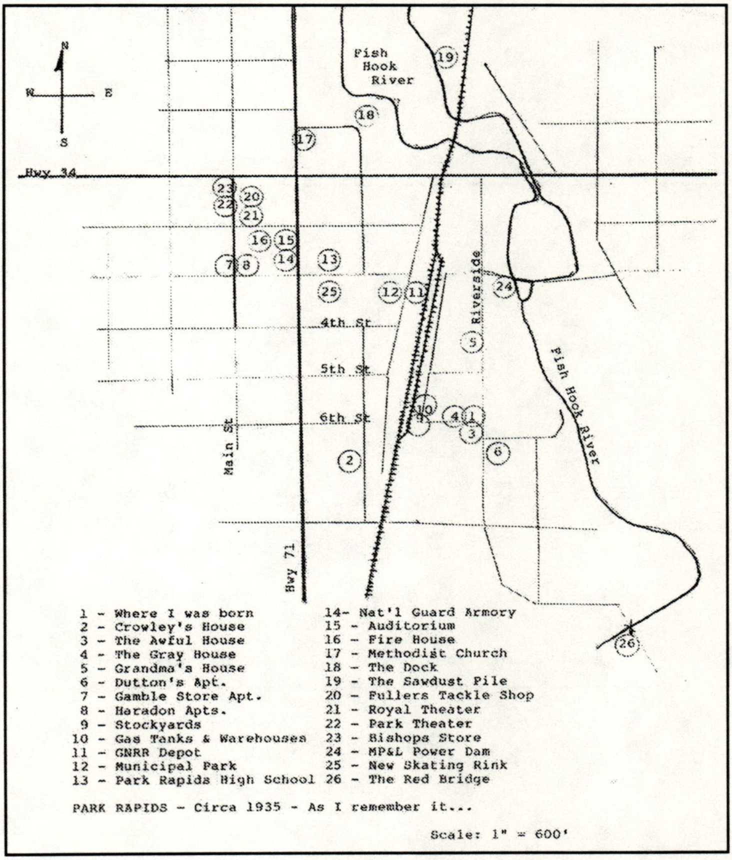
N
W
E
S
Fish Hook River
Hwy 34
Riverside
4th St
5th St
6th St
Main St
Hwy 71
Fish Hook River
1 - Where I was born
2 - Crowley's House
3 - The Awful House
4 - The Gray House
5 - Grandma's House
6 - Dutton's Apt.
7 - Gamble Store Apt.
8 - Haradon Apts.
9 - Stockyards
10 - Gas Tanks & Warehouses
11 - GNRR Depot
12 - Municipal Park
13 - Park Rapids High School
14- Nat'l Guard Armory
15 - Auditorium
16 - Fire House
17 - Methodist Church
18 - The Dock
19 - The Sawdust Pile
20 - Fullers Tackle Shop
21 - Royal Theater
22 - Park Theater
23 - Bishops Store
24 - MP&L Power Dam
25 - New Skating Rink
26 - The Red Bridge
PARK RAPIDS - Circa 1935 - As I remember it...
Scale: 1" = 600'

Don's Map

Dons House

Don 1928

Sonny & Dodie

Eula, Wen, Me 1935

Fatty & I grey house 1936

Birthday Party 1936

Eula, Mom, Wen & Me 1939

Grandma Black at the house on Riverside 1943

Chapter III
The Great Depression

"We have not now the strength which in old days moved earth and heaven; that which we are, we are, one equal temper of heroic hearts, made weak by time and fate, but strong in will. To strive, to seek, to find and not to yield."

Tennyson from Ulysses

The stock market crashed in 1929 and overnight, the Roaring Twenties came to an end and gave way to the iron grip of the Great Depression. This rare and terrible economic event wrapped the country in its tentacles until the United States entered World War II in 1941. On Wall Street, many over-extended investors literally leapt from the windows of their skyscraper offices or blew their brains out rather than face the impossible debts that they had accumulated by margin calls as stock prices plummeted.

Unemployment rates soared to over 25% across the country as businesses closed, families lost their savings and their homes and farms, banks closed and then failed and mortgage foreclosures became the order of the day. Soon after, we lost Dad and our family took on the challenges related to overnight loss of income and the Great Depression. How did it affect us? In these ways:

There were few, if any, jobs to be had. Dad had a good job until his untimely death in 1930. Many others lost their jobs and could not find work. Out of desperation, many men left their homes and families and traveled all over the U.S. looking for employment. How did they pay for all of this travel? Most did not. They hitchhiked and they traveled on freight trains from one city to another. 'Riding the rails' this was called. It was illegal, but railroad authorities generally turned a blind eye to these down-and-out, destitute men who traveled the country in empty boxcars. They camped along the railroad right-of-way and went from house to house in the towns asking for handouts. We called them 'bums', not meant to be a derogatory term. Others called them 'tramps' or 'hobos'. The kindest term was 'transient', and we saw a lot of them regardless of what they were called. Northern Minnesota may have been a popular destination for these unfortunates because of the prospect of finding logging jobs in the lumber camps of the north woods. Others went west trying to find work as farm laborers or ranch hands. They were all on the move and were extremely lucky to find work of any kind. Those were good days to be self employed and/or financially secure. We were neither.

Since we lived so close to the railroad tracks and its small switchyard, we had frequent contact with these dirty, ragged yet proud men from the cities across America. They would come to our door, hat or cap in hand asking for food.

Even in our near-poverty condition, Mom never turned them away, nor did she ever let them inside the house. She might ask them to chop some wood or do some other kind of chore that needed doing and then she would bring them a plate of food. Many times I would sit on the front porch as they wolfed down their free meal. Other times, my friends and I would come across one of their camps by the railroad tracks or by the river where we would stop and talk to them by their campfire. They were kindly men and talked to us about their travels and about their families. Never did we feel threatened or at risk in any way. Charge it up to our naivete if you will but I believe that it was just a different era where there was trust amongst strangers and kidnapping and assaults against children were rarely heard of.

It wasn't long after the start of the Depression that the Federal Government tried its hand at solving the nation's problems. Herbert Hoover was President then and for whatever reason was unsuccessful at turning the country's economy around. Franklin Delano Roosevelt followed Hoover into the White House and is generally given credit for ending the Depression. Although some of his three-letter programs did have a positive effect on the country, I believe that it was World War II that actually ended the Depression. Industrial activity exploded in the '40s in order to meet the demand for arms and munitions and to rebuild our Army and Navy. And, we helped to re-arm our allies. All of this pumped dollars and jobs into the economy and ended the Depression.

In the '30s, the U.S. economy was hitting rock bottom and Europe and the U.S. were trying, successfully, to ignore Hitler and Mussolini in Europe and Africa as well as Japanese expansionism in the Pacific, thereby setting the stage for World War II. It was then that Roosevelt introduced his New Deal to the Americans. Some of his policies worked for a time; others such as Social Security and the Federal Income Tax are still with us. Lucky us!

One of his programs that worked quite well and one that we saw first-hand in northern Minnesota was the establishment of the Civilian Conservation Corps or CCC. This was a plan whereby young unemployed men from the cities were encouraged to enlist in the CCC program , were given uniforms and small salaries and were sent to National and State Parks and forests across the country. There they built their own camps generally in wilderness settings and were paid to work on improvement projects of various kinds. Mostly they built roads and bridges and visitor facilities in the national parks. The program took kids off the streets of New York, Philadelphia, Chicago and other large cities that were stricken by the Depression and sent them throughout the country. The kids got to see, most for the first time, life outside of the city, the great out-of-doors and the wonders of the west. The results of their efforts can still be seen. Many of the older facilities at Yellowstone and Glacier Parks were built by the CCCs. Boys in camps near Park Rapids did most of their work in Itasca State Park., building roads, camp grounds and other facilities.

Trainloads of CCC recruits would pass through town on their way to the camps. I don't think that I ever knew how many CCC camps were built around PR but there were enough that they held basketball games and tournaments amongst the camps at the Armory in Park Rapids. We didn't see them on Main Street very often; they were generally kept quite busy at the camps. But even so, they created quite a bit of interest amongst the young ladies of Park Rapids. They were nice young men; well behaved, and the results of their toil remain and will remain for decades to come.

Another of the three-letter programs that produced

lasting results was the WPA or the Works Progress Administration. Like the CCC, the WPA provided government funded jobs for the unemployed. WPA workers built Post Offices and other municipal projects in the towns and cities. Many, if not most, are still standing and in daily use. These two programs were likely prototypes for Kennedy's Peace Corp established in later years. The WPA was the butt of many jokes generally symbolized by a man leaning on a shovel. While not renowned for efficiency and productivity, the WPA never-the-less provided dignified work and lasting results.

And, there was the NRA, the National Recovery Act, one of the first safety-net programs. Some called it relief, and it was designed to provide food and clothing to those who requested that assistance.

Mom was too proud to ask for help from any of the government relief oriented programs. We always had enough to eat. Some of my classmates did not. I wore hand-me-down clothes and two episodes will always remain in my memory. I was sent to First Grade on one of the first cold days in the late fall in a green girl's coat with a brown fur collar. After being teased mercilessly on the play ground for wearing girl's clothing, I refused to wear the coat ever again. Mom and Eula worked together to remake a coat that appeared from somewhere into a warm coat that a boy would be proud to wear and I was warm for the rest of that winter.

A few years later, Eula made a hood-like cap for me out of fake fur that tied under the chin. The result was similar; after one day of being called girl's names on the playground, the fur hood was banished, the treasury was raided and I was presented with an imitation leather helmet with goggles, very 'in' at the time, and all was well again. One way or another, I was always warmly dressed.

In second grade, I became very ill, scarlet fever I think. Whatever it was it was contagious and Dr. Houston quarantined our house for a few weeks (doctors made house calls in those days) and I missed so much school that it was questionable if I would be allowed to remain with my class. During that time, one of our neighbors, the Millers, brought us a sack of groceries. There were oranges and grapefruit, the first that I had ever tasted. There was also grape juice, another first. This was an act of charity and thoughtfulness that I will always remember and was very welcome.

Another event of that era that I haven't mentioned until now was Prohibition. Prohibition, a Federal law, made the sale and even the possession of alcoholic beverages illegal. It was instituted in the 1920s and didn't end until late in 1933. With Prohibition came crime with bootlegging and smuggling. With crime came the mob, most of whom operated out of the big cities like New York, Boston and Philadelphia. Chicago had a large population of mobsters and bootlegging and smuggling and some of them found their way up to St. Paul, and yes, although later, even up as far as Park Rapids. At this point I will be relating rumor more than fact, because at my tender age then, I heard some of the rumors but had no way of establishing facts.

I recall, while listening in on adult conversations, stories of strange airplanes that flew into the area at night and landed in some of the outlying fields. They were supposedly carrying bootleg booze from Canada. I heard other stories of local folks making bathtub gin and other such goodies.

One summer, Wen did some yard work for two families who summered on Fish Hook Lake. He told of seeing a tommy gun lying on a bed in one of the cabins. These were families who were rumored to be affiliated with the

Chicago and St. Paul mobs. In fact, one of the individuals supposedly took part in the St. Valentine's Day Massacre, a much publicized mob killing in the late 20s. Years later when I was running my resort paper route, both of these families were my customers. They were very nice people to deal with, but I always hated to collect from one of the men who seemed to be a very cold individual indeed.

One humorous story that has its roots in Prohibition occurred when I was in junior high school. It was rumored that Charlie Green had developed his own supply of homemade adult beverages. During Christmas of the year in question, our Methodist Sunday school class was participating in the annual Christmas Pageant. My good friend Chuck Green brought a jar of his dad's 'grape juice' to the final rehearsal just prior to the pageant itself. Chuck shared his 'grape juice' with many members of the pageant cast; it was very good. It certainly tasted like grape juice. The Methodist pageant that Christmas was memorable, with forgotten and substituted lines being the very least of the departures from the planned production. Mercifully, the pageant came to an appropriate end when 'Joseph' tipped over the Christmas Tree.

Chapter IV

There Were Hot Times…

"I would rather be ashes than dust; I would rather my spark should burn out in a brilliant blaze than it should be stifled in dry rot. I would rather be a meteor, every atom of me in magnificent glow, than a sleepy and permanent plant. Mans chief purpose is to live not exist; I shall not waste my days trying to prolong them. I shall use my time."

Jack London

Fires were not uncommon when I was growing up in Park Rapids: forest fires, fires in commercial buildings and especially home fires.

Nearly all of the residences in Northern Minnesota are of frame construction and many of them were already quite old in the 1930s. A few were little more than shacks and some were shacks. In those days, most houses were heated by wood burning stoves. Smoke from the burning of wood contains highly flammable particles, creosote, which, over time, will accumulate on the inside of stove pipes and chimneys, the same pitch-like material that can be found in the flues of today's wood burning fireplaces. Back then, when enough of this flammable material had accumulated, it would sometimes ignite causing what we called a 'chimney fire'. This type of fire can be very dangerous because creosote will burn at temperatures as high as 2,000 degrees. These temperatures would heat up the stove pipe which generally was poorly insulated from the walls and ceilings through which it had to pass. Or, the old chimney, even if it was brick, might leak through the side walls causing adjacent material to ignite resulting in a full fledged house fire. This type of fire was most likely to occur during a cold winter night when the heating stove was working the hardest and the stoves and stovepipes were the hottest.

Park Rapids had, and probably still has, a volunteer fire department. Volunteers lived at home and were summoned to a fire by a siren located at the fire station across from the library. When we heard the siren at night, we would rush outside to look for the red glow in the sky which would give us some idea of the fire's location and maybe even whose house was burning. This fire siren could be heard all over town. But it always took some time for the volunteers to get dressed and make their way to the station or directly to the fire. So, by the time the firemen arrived at the fire, it would probably have a good head start. Damage to homes due to fires was frequently severe and often resulted in complete loss of the structure. I can still feel the awesome dread when the siren was heard late on a cold winter night and we would wonder whose home might be in danger. .

We had a chimney fire over our kitchen stove one summer. It happened in the daytime so that we were able to detect it and to report it early. The fire truck arrived and extinguished the fire before any damage was done. We were very lucky!

Two large fires stand out in my memory. One was the Gage Block fire that destroyed an entire block of buildings at the south end of Main Street. The fire started in the early evening and burned well into the night. It was too large for our fire fighters to control, even with the help of fire units that came from towns as far away as Verndale. They could only keep it from spreading. We, of course, ran to the fire to watch the spectacle. The new Post Office built by the WPA, was built on one corner of the old Gage block after the remnants of the old buildings were removed.

The other fire that I remember, had a much greater impact on my young life. That night, we heard the siren, ran outside to look and saw a huge red glow in the sky in the direction of the school. I said, "I hope it's the school!" and much to my chagrin, it was. Again, we ran across the railroad tracks to watch the fire.

Both high school and grade schools shared the same two story brick building. It was the high school end of the building that was destroyed. Consequently, the high school kids took over the grade school rooms and we grade school students were sent to various other buildings around town to attend classes until the new (at that time) high school was completed. Fourth and fifth grade classes went to the American Legion Building near the old concrete water tower, a long walk from home. Sixth graders went to class in the Community Club Rooms above the fire station. We could really hear the fire siren when it called! Some of the lower grades went to churches around town.

The new school was finished in time for my class to start junior high and to finish senior high there. We considered ourselves to be very lucky to be the first class to occupy the new building.

Park Rapids, surrounded by forests, had its share of forest fires. These fires were fought by volunteers led by a few men from the local Forest Service on the west edge of town. When the size of the fire exceeded the capability of the volunteers, and because many of the men from PR were away at war, Mr. Kirkvold, the forest ranger, would come to the high school to ask for help. What red blooded junior or senior boy would elect to stay in class on a nice Spring or Fall day when given the opportunity to go play in the woods?

Consequently, my friends and I were able to participate in fighting and helping to control a few forest fires around Park Rapids. Actually, fighting fire is not much fun and is mostly a lot of hard work, as we soon learned. Our tools were mostly shovels and brush hooks, the latter a wicked looking axe-like weapon with a curved steel blade that a medieval executioner might envy. These tools were used to dig containing trenches around the fire and to remove flammable material from the fire's perimeter. If we were lucky, we got to use a water dispensing device called a 'trombone'. This device was a water filled five gallon tank carried on our back with a hand operated pump, the trombone. The only disadvantage, besides being heavy and clumsy, was that we had to find a stream or pond in which to refill it when the water supply was exhausted. This of course took the fire fighter away from the fire-line so that shovels and brush hooks were probably more efficient and to be preferred, although not as much fun.

Fighting forest fire is not without its danger. When on the fire-line, we always had to be aware of the location of the fire and the direction and strength of the wind. This was not always easy to do because of confusion and noise and concentrations of smoke on the down wind side of the fire.

If the wind caused the fire to leap from the ground into the tops of the trees, a crown fire, it was possible for the fire to travel from tree to tree as fast or faster than a man can run. On one such occasion, we were forced to flee, at top speed, to an open space with the fire at our heels.

Another time, late at night, with the fire contained but still dangerous, a group of us were resting near the fire line when a gust of wind moved the flames into a large pine tree just inside the perimeter. The tree literally exploded. Quite spectacular.

Surprisingly, these Minnesota experiences helped me during Navy fire fighting training at boot camp. I was the only one in our company who knew how to quickly start and run a 'handy billy' a small, portable, gasoline powered pump. You never know when a skill may come in handy in later days and under different circumstances.

Chapter V

The Railroad And Other Playgrounds

"One hour of life, crowded to the full with glorious action, and filled with noble risks, is worth whole years of those mean observances of paltry decorum, in which men steal through existence, like sluggish waters through a marsh,without honour or observation.

Sir Walter Scott

You could say that we lived on the wrong side of the tracks and you wouldn't be far wrong. Actually, the Fish Hook River was the unofficial dividing line between the west side and the east side of town, so we made it on the 'right side of town', but just barely. Never the less, the Great Northern Railroad played an important role in our lives in more ways than one.

Dad worked for the Great Northern when we first moved to PR and worked there until his death. It was an easy walk to work for Dad and after he died, we remained in the same area, probably because of familiarity. From the Gray House, when any of our family went to school or went to town, we had to walk across the railroad tracks; and the tracks and the area surrounding them was one of my playgrounds.

We always lived close to the railroad tracks, to the stockyards, to the river and to the open country southeast of town. What kid today could hope to live next to so many different places to play? Did we get into trouble? Oh yes! Did we have fun? Always! Did we survive? Of course, but not without a lot of bumps and bruises and not without a few close calls. But first, let me tell you about the railroad tracks.

There were always strings of rail cars parked on the various sidings: box cars, flat cars, tank cars, cattle cars and gondola cars. Near the depot there was a large wooden water tower with a large steel spout that could be lowered by a long chain to dispense water to the steam locomotives. (It was years before we ever saw one of the new diesel-electric locomotives.) This tower grew incredible icicles in the winter. There were bulk gasoline storage facilities along one of the sidings each with a row of large gasoline storage tanks. Next to them were some coal storage sheds and a couple of abandoned warehouses. The stockyards were close to our house and on our side of the tracks. On the west side were stacks of telephone and power poles to be used in line construction and more rail sidings. This was one of our playgrounds.

The stockyards were primary in our play because they were active and frequently contained various types of livestock: cattle, pigs and sheep mostly. We thought that the animals were there for us to ride, which we did frequently when we didn't get caught and chased away.

One night after school with a new pen of sheep resident, my friends, and I resplendent in a new pair of overalls, let a few sheep out of their pen into one of the transfer chutes and proceeded to have our own little rodeo. It didn't take long for my mount to dump me into a particularly murky puddle of water and you-know-what. Needless to say, I was not welcomed with open arms at supper that night.

Another stockyard sport, one in which I excelled, was fence walking. The pens were built of two-by-eight planks fastened to eight-inch poles. The game was to walk along the 1-3/4 inch edge of the fence and to walk as far as you could. It wasn't long before we could walk around the entire stockyard without falling. There were a few falls of course, into the pens or off to the outside. The falls that were both memorable as well as painful were those where ones feet slipped and one ended up a-straddle of the fence. After we were tired of fence walking, we would retire to the sloped roofs of the sheds to relax and just watch the animals or to enjoy the sun and the day. I can still feel the warm smoothness of the roof planks on my bare feet (we generally went barefoot the entire summer) and it makes my toes curl just thinking about it.

Less often, we played in, on and around the rail cars parked on the sidings. It was fun to run along the tops of the boxcars jumping from one car to the next, just like in the cowboy shows that we watched on Saturday afternoons at the Royal Theater. If there were boxcars that were unlocked, and they generally were, we would climb inside and play. We had to be alert to the presence of a switch engine, to any sounds of the car being coupled and being made up into a train to be sure that we were not trapped inside. We generally stayed away from the flat cars; it was too easy to be seen by the railroad workers who would chase us away. Tank cars were to be avoided because they were generally filled with smelly stuff and were slippery on top. Gondola cars were hard to get into and harder to get out of so we stayed away from those also.

The vacant warehouses were fair game although they were dark and spooky and could be dangerous. My friend Don Town gave us a scare one day at the gasoline bulk station. The station had a raised wooden platform with three or four swivel pipes for unloading gasoline from the bulk tanks into tank trucks for transport to the filling stations downtown. These pipes generally had a little gasoline left in the spout after the loading operation was completed. Don liked the smell of gasoline and this day took to lying on the platform with his nose in the spout smelling the gas. Shortly, we noticed that Don wasn't moving. We pulled him away from the spout, called parents who in turn called for assistance. Firemen arrived and Don was revived after some artificial respiration. Needless to say, he didn't do that again.

These large gasoline tanks were a source of worry to my young mind. Many nights, I would finish my prayers with "…and please God, don't let the gas tanks explode tonight". He must have heard me because they never did.

The attraction of the railroad was not limited to the sidings and tracks near our house, however. As we grew older and were able to venture farther from home, we included two railroad bridges that were fairly close by. One crossed the Straight River about four miles south of town and is no longer there. It, like all of the other railroad tracks and features were removed some years ago when Great Northern withdrew rail service from Park Rapids. The other bridge across the Fish Hook River still stands although it is now part of a bicycle path that goes from Park Rapids to Walker and perhaps beyond. But back then, we spent many happy hours playing on those two bridges. In the summer, we would dive from the bridge railing into the Fish Hook River. We had to be a little careful because there were old pilings just beneath the river surface near the ends of the bridge. They were generally clearly visible so easily avoided.

Another exciting adventure was to climb underneath either bridge as a train approached. We would climb as close to the underside of the tracks as possible. When the train passed over the bridge, the entire structure would sway and shake and the roar of the train was deafening. Not dangerous, but very exciting.

Then there were other mundane activities such as putting pennies on the tracks so the train would smash them into interesting shapes as it passed over. My cousin Leo put a shotgun shell on the track one day. Now that was really exciting! No one got hurt.

Much later, in high school, a few of us would sometimes jump into an open box car as the train was leaving PR and would ride it to Dorset or to Nevis depending on where it slowed down enough for us to jump off. We would then hitch hike home. On one such day, the car that we chose was occupied by a transient, a bum, or a hobo; you select the term. By the time we realized that we were not alone, the train was moving too fast for us to leave safely. So we coexisted with our passenger friend who was probably as uncomfortable as we were, until we reached Dorset where we parted company as soon as the train slowed down sufficiently.

Another time, my good friend Bill Skelton, who was uncannily accurate with a slingshot hit a pheasant in the head with a lump of coal from the doorway of our moving boxcar. Lucky? Perhaps, but I prefer to think that is was yet another demonstration of Bill's well developed hand-eye coordination.

The open fields and woods south of town were settings for many happy days and adventures. 'Going for a hike' meant heading for the woods via the Red Bridge or the open fields on the west side of the river. There were the woods themselves and a couple of abandoned farms to explore. One of the farms had a silo that we could climb to the top, either on the inside or the outside of the silo. The vacant farmhouses had remnants of furniture and old papers to be examined. Once we stopped at the run-down house of "One Eared Smith" south of town. He was an elderly recluse who lived alone and had only one ear, the other supposedly bitten off by his horse some years before. He was also rumored to be a graduate from an Eastern law school, and those few who had been inside his house confirmed that the small dwelling had shelves full of law books. We always returned home from these hikes tired and dirty and sometimes wet from crossing the river and thoroughly pleased with the day.

I recall one such day when my faithful dog Fatty, a mongrel that had Fox Terrier ancestry but looked a little like a Border Collie, and I were hiking by ourselves. Passing through a recently cut-over field with piles of slashings everywhere, Fatty disappeared under a pile of slashings from which growls and yelps and other sounds of animal strife emanated. Envisioning an encounter with a bear, at least, and fearing for Fatty's welfare, I grasped his tail and pulled him from beneath the pile. Grasped between his jaws was a large and very smelly skunk which Fatty immediately and proudly dispatched. By this time, Fatty, the skunk and I all smelled alike. So with nothing more to lose, and as a souvenir of the skirmish, I removed the skunk's tail with my pocket knife, tucked it under my belt and headed for home. Eula and I lived in the Gamble Store apartment at that time. In spite of what people say, tomato juice, even in large quantities is not really effective in removing skunk musk especially in doses that we had been exposed to. Fatty and I were both personae-non-grata for a number of days. Oh yes!

One other ill-advised episode comes to mind. Years later, one of the older high school kids, Jim Wien and my cousin Leo, I think, and I were hiking down by the river on a cool day in early spring. While hiking near the river we came across a large hen turkey that had probably escaped from Gutzler's turkey farm not far away. In the interest of returning the turkey to its home we pursued the bird across the river a number of times. Unfortunately, in the melee, the poor bird lost its head, literally. It was not I, but Jim, who did the dastardly deed. What to do? In the spirit of conservation, we cleaned the bird as best we could (with a nail file as I remember) and packed the carcass away in a snow bank. The very next Saturday, we returned with all of the necessities for a roast turkey feast. However, our good intentions exceeded our skills. The bird, turned on a spit over an open fire, was charred on the outside and quite raw on the inside. Alas, the poor foul had died in vain.

If I wax nostalgic about these events, it is not by chance. These were good days that I love to relive in the telling to my children and grandchildren as often as they will listen and with only the least bit of enhancement. It is not possible to have been poor with a childhood such as mine and with playgrounds such as these. Lucky, lucky me!

Chapter VI

A River Runs Through

"Time is but a stream I go fishing in; I drink at it, but while I drink, I see sandy bottom and detect how shallow it is. It's then the current slides away and Eternity remains."
Thoreau

I don't think that anyone has ever paddled a canoe from Park Rapids to the Gulf of Mexico. I don't believe that anyone has, but they could. In fact, they could start at Island Lake, north of PR, paddle into Eagle Lake then into Potato Lake, then into the Potato River into Fish Hook Lake and hence into Fish Hook River. One would have to portage over the power dam in Park Rapids and follow the Fish Hook River until it is joined by the Straight River (good trout fishing) and becomes the Shell River. After a few miles, the Shell River joins the Crow Wing River near Huntersville. Follow the Crow Wing for a day or two and you will meet the Mighty Mississippi just southwest of Brainerd. From there you just go with the flow, and if you stay with it, after a number of portages and taking care to dodge tug boats and barges you will eventually reach New Orleans, and just beyond, the Gulf of Mexico. I wonder why no one has tried this; it would be an incredible adventure. If Bill and/or Bob and I had it all to do over again, maybe we would give it a try. I wonder.

But getting back to Fish Hook Lake; some mapmaker got a little mixed up in its naming. Fish Hook Lake is shaped like a Potato and Potato Lake is shaped like a fish hook, more or less. But whatever its shape and name, Fish Hook Lake and more importantly, its river, played a major role in my life. We swam in it. We fished it. We canoed on it. We skated on it above the dam and rode ice flows on it below the dam. We rode our sleds and our primitive skis on the hills along its banks. We hiked along its shores and we picnicked, but whatever we did, we had fun.

I learned to swim in the river. When I was eight or nine years old, Mom was hired as matron at the public swimming beach in Park Rapids: we called it 'the Dock'. Her job was to pass out baskets for the swimmers to keep their clothes and belongings in while they were swimming, to sell candy and pop and to keep a modicum of law and order amongst the kids. She and I walked to the Dock at nine o'clock each morning in the summer and walked home at nine o'clock in the evening. Between those hours, while Mom worked, I taught myself to swim and to dive from the springboard and from the tower. While perfecting the latter skill one evening, I executed one of the worlds most ungainly and painful bellyflops. That event taught me to keep my eyes open until my body's attitude prior to entry into the water was well established.

Also working at the Dock that summer was a very nice

man named Chuck Hendricks who ran several summer craft programs for the kids. With his help, I made a toy sailboat and sailed it in the river; and he taught me how to play ping pong. What a summer that was; swimming and lying in the warm sand and hanging out with my friends, all day, every day!

Later in my life, our scoutmaster and track coach, Quentin Jones, encouraged me to become a Red Cross Junior Life Guard; and still later while attending college in Bemidji, I qualified as a Red Cross Life Guard and Swimming and Life Saving Instructor. These qualifications served me well as I worked a few summers for the County, teaching swimming and life saving in Park Rapids and at other beaches in Hubbard County. What a great summer job!

One summer while in high school, someone abandoned an old canvas covered canoe at the Dock. The canvas had been slashed with a knife, so the Dock manager at that time, gave the canoe to Bob and to me. We patched it and painted it red, made two paddles out of orange crate panels and broom sticks and *voila*, we had water transport that we enjoyed for a couple of years. A few years later, we acquired another fixer-upper canoe, a green one this time. I will never forget that feeling of freedom when we were the first watercraft on the river in the spring when there was still a lot of ice along the shores. I would paddle and Bill would pick off muskrats from the edges of the ice with his slingshot.

Before the canoe, I had access to a small, flat-bottomed skiff about six feet long. It was new and it was also painted green and had been made by "Windy" Anderson who kept a carpenter shop in the old Germania Hall on the river. It belonged to "Windy" but it was mine to use any time I wanted it.

During final exams my freshman year in high school, I had a few hours between tests, so I went fishing. There was an old abandoned sawmill on the east bank of the river, not far from the Dock. A huge pile of sawdust, chips and shavings extended down from the mill into the river. It was a treacherous place because the water-soaked sawdust acted somewhat like quicksand. We kids sometimes played on the sawdust pile, but we were always careful to stay away from the line where the water and the sawdust met. One day a cow became mired in that no-mans-land and had to be removed by a truck pulling on a rope wrapped around the cow's horns. But, I digress.

That morning I rowed my little boat over to the sawdust pile and began casting a medium-sized Daredevil. For you non-fisher folk, a Daredevil is a red and white striped spoon with a treble hook that is murderous for Northern Pike. I was casting my Daredevil toward an old tree-stump that was partially covered by water and about twenty yards from the sawdust pile. As I was retrieving a cast, my spoon jerked to a stop. Convinced that I had snagged the stump or one of its roots, I pulled hard on the rod and my snag appeared to come free, and I reeled it in with no resistance. However, as it came closer to the boat I couldn't see it when it should have been visible to me. As I reeled in the last few feet of line, I looked over the side of the boat and out of the black depths of the river there arose a fish larger than I had ever seen before, with my Daredevil hanging precariously from its mouth by only one hook. I didn't own a landing net or a gaff hook, so slowly taking the slack out of the line, I gingerly reached for the spoon and grasping it, with a mighty heave, hauled the fish into the boat. The fish wasn't having any of this however; and immediately flopped out of the other side. Miraculously, it was still attached to my line. I repeated the process and it once again flopped out of the other side of the boat and once again remained hooked by my Daredevil. I felt that my luck was not going to continue, so the next time I got it into the boat, I pounced on the fish and held it to the bottom. It was a good thing too, because at that moment, the hook fell loose. I did have a stringer in my small tackle box, so I carefully removed it with one hand, ran it through the fish's gills and tied the stringer to my leg. Wherever that fish and I were going from that moment on, we were going together!

Fullers Tackle Shop on Main Street kept a large tray of ice in their store window for the purpose of displaying fish that local fisherman were proud of. I was very proud of this fish, so with the stringer and my fish slung across my back, we headed for Main Street and Fullers. It turned out to weigh 12 pounds 12 ounces, not large by some standards, but huge by mine; a female Northern Pike that I shall never forget.

As I mentioned earlier, I worked as life guard at the swimming beach for a few summers. It was normally a quiet, uneventful job. I taught swimming and life saving classes and worked on my tan. (As a tanning lotion, we mixed iodine and Johnson's Baby Oil. It worked really well.) I spent most of my time sitting on my lifeguard's perch watching after the water rats and other swimmers. The water rats were a dozen or so kids between eight and ten years old who seemed to live at the Dock whenever it was open for swimming. They were all good friends, helped me with some of my chores and generally stayed out of trouble.

Late one afternoon, I was sitting in the lifeguard's chair and wearing a borrowed bathing suit, as all of mine were wet from classes, and my day was nearly over. I was watching the swimmers, most of whom I knew well and knew what to expect from them. A carload of adult tourists arrived at about that time and went into the bathhouse to change. The first one out was a big guy who turned out to be a college football player. He charged into the water, took a few strokes, found that he couldn't touch bottom and proceeded to drown. He was about twenty feet from my perch; an easy rescue. I reached for the life-ring that always hung from the side of my chair and threw it towards the drowning man. I should have checked it when I went on duty, but I hadn't. The water rats had been playing with it, had tangled the line and it wouldn't reach my man.

No sweat! Normally, I would have jumped into the water, made an underwater approach to his rear, put him in a cross-chest carry and brought him into shore. However, he was in a perfect position for a dive from the perch, passing underneath him and coming up from his rear. Simple, right? Wrong! As I dove into the water, my too large, borrowed swim trunks went to my ankles. There I was, directly beneath him, with his thrashing feet in my face as I frantically tried to get my trunks up where they belonged. By the time I had my bare bod sufficiently covered and I had surfaced, my victim had turned around so that I came up right in front of him. He immediately grabbed for me. A bear hug from the big guy at that moment would not have been good. Fortunately, my Red Cross training became automatic, and I parried his grab with a straight right arm to his left shoulder, ducked under his right arm and got my arm across his chest and tugged him onto my hip. One problem; he was so big and heavy that my head was completely under water. I didn't dare release my hold on him, but I did manage to get my head up for a breath every three or four strokes. We didn't have far to go and he was a model victim once I had him under control, so in a short time we were sitting side-by-side in shallow water. He was gasping for breath and I was chuckling over the humorous (to me) events a few moments before. He didn't seem to think that it was that funny.

I didn't have to rescue very many people during those years, mostly kids, but as I remember, no one ever said thank you.

The passing of summer and the coming of winter did not end our river activities; *au contraire.* For many years the town fathers kept a skating rink on the river near the Dock. They kept it plowed, although we kids helped with the shoveling as well. They flooded it periodically to keep it smooth using a pumper from the Fire Department. It was one of the things that we did after school, skating until the warming house closed or when it was too dark to see. Later this rink was moved to a location across the street from the High School and near the Park. This rink was lighted and had a better warming house. We boys all had hockey skates, although we seldom played hockey; the girls all had figure skates, and some even had figures.

But the best skating was on the river as soon as the ice was relatively safe and before the snow fell. There was an unofficial contest amongst the skaters in PR to be the first to skate up the river and around Fish Hook Lake; about a ten mile round trip if you went all the way. Those years when the snow fell late and the river froze early, we were exposed to skating heaven. Imagine being able to skate for miles as fast as you were able on ice as smooth as glass and so transparent that you could see the weeds and the fish in shallow water. In fact that was another fun thing that we did; we would locate big fish in the shallows, generally on the north side of the lake and would chase them, keeping contact visually through the ice. The entire feeling was one of flying on ice.

Skating the river this early in the season was not

without its risks because we skated on ice that was sometimes only marginally safe in some places, especially near the Point where the Fish Hook River emptied out of Fish Hook Lake. The current there kept a small area free of ice or at least thin in spots well into the winter. While there were many wet feet and the occasional wet body, there were no fatalities although there was one episode that nearly ended in disaster. Chuck Williams and another skater, Danny Farr I believe, had skated up to the lake after school and were returning after dark. Both fell through the ice and were able to help each other out of the water. It was very cold, so that by the time they had skated the two miles back to town, their clothes were frozen stiff and they were starting to freeze. As I recall, Chuck spent a night in the hospital, although I may be confusing this with another incident involving Chuck and Danny. Both were duck hunting on a small lake northwest of town using a borrowed duck boat. The old boat began to leak and sank before they could get back to shore. Although the water was not very deep, they were able to swim a short distance and then to break through thin ice as they waded a hundred yards or so to shore. It was dark by this time and they began walking towards a farmhouse. Chuck had taken off some of his clothing while in the water and now was starting to freeze. His hand froze to Danny's shoulder as Danny led the way to the farmhouse and to warmth and safety. There are times in that country when there is a very narrow difference between adventure and disaster. Fortunately this one remained in the adventure category.

One year, our senior year in high school I think, Bill Skelton, Louise Reynolds and I were competing for "first around the lake" bragging rights and shared one such adventure. As it turned out, we were a little too early in the season. We had made it to the northeast corner of the lake when a wind began to blow and combined with the young, thin ice caused the ice to begin to break up. We had been skating about a hundred yards from shore because there was occasionally open water near the shore. We suddenly found ourselves on a large sheet of ice with an ever widening gap between our ice sheet and the main body of ice. There was no going back at this point. The large ice flow that we shared was drifting toward the shore but appeared that it wasn't going to make it all the way. As we kept moving on the ice, the ice flow drifted to within a few yards of a boat dock that had not yet been removed from the lake. One by one and skating as fast as we could we jumped over the open water onto the dock. Safe at last! But, the adventure was not quite over. It was getting dark, we were about ten miles from town, near an infrequently traveled road and with nothing but our skates and skate sox to wear on our feet. We had left our boots at the Dock in PR. Using our ingrained 'survival instincts' we stripped bark from a birch tree, stuffed the bark into the bottoms of our skate sox and set forth. After getting to a road with a little more traffic, we were able to hitch-hike back to town and to our boots. Only our skate sox did not survive.

There are many Long Lakes in Minnesota, and Park Rapids has one of its own: a beautiful lake about nine miles long that averages about a mile in width. Its north end is about three miles east of PR off Highway 34 and the lake runs south to the town of Hubbard. On one of those wonderful early winter days when the ice was thick and with scarcely any snow on its surface, Bill's dad drove Bill and I to Hubbard with our ice-kites. We had made these kites from old sheets fastened to a diamond shaped wooden frame, with dimensions of about six feet by four feet. There was a light wind blowing straight out of the south that day. With the kites across our backs we were blown at moderate speeds north towards the north end of the lake. But when we tacked at an angle to the wind, as one might in a sailboat, we reached seemingly incredible speeds. We went so fast that our ankles became fatigued and sore as we raced across ice that had seemed smooth when we started. Too soon, we reached the north end of the lake. What a ride! We never did it again, Why not? I can't tell you. Maybe there were too many other things to do; I don't know.

But, getting back to ice flows. Below the power dam in PR is a pond about a hundred yards across that is quite deep in places and shallow in others. This was a great place to fish for sunfish, bluegills and bullheads in the summer. But in the winter the pond was generally covered by a thin sheet of ice except for where the water emerged from the power plant generators. In the early spring, it was possible to break off small sheets of ice, large enough to hold a few people. We would then pole these flows on down the river as far as the ice flows would allow. Where the river exited the pond it probably averaged three feet in depth and five to ten yards in width.

On one such sunny day in the early spring, three or four of us, Bill, Lowell Mason, and I think Duane Henry, and I were busy breaking off an ice flow for a voyage down the river. I had broken off a likely sheet of ice and was poling it to shore to pick up passengers when it broke into two pieces. I stepped onto the largest piece which promptly broke again. I thought that I was over the deep part of the pond and didn't want to fall in with the chance of becoming trapped under the ice. So, I lay down on what ice remained, and slithered across it toward shore. I arrived soaking wet much to the enjoyment of my so-called friends who had known all along that I was in the shallow part of the pond. But did they tell me that? Noooooooooo!

We did eventually secure an appropriately sized ice craft and proceeded down the river to the Red Bridge. Abandoning our craft there. We walked back to town, our pant legs frozen stiff, but tired and happy. Why didn't we catch pneumonia or at least a cold? I can't guess.

Let me regale you with one more Bill and Don adventure. One day during Christmas vacation, I think it was, Bill and I were skating on the river a couple of hundred yards above the Dock. It was about noon when we skated up to Danny Farr's fish house. For you folks from the dry parts of the country, a Minnesota fish house is a small shack that is generally built to seat two fishermen around a two foot square hole in the floor. There are no windows in these heated shacks so they are also called 'dark houses' and because the shack has no windows, one can see for some distance into the water. It is illegal to fish with a hook and line from a dark house, but it is legal to use a decoy to lure a fish into view and then to spear it. Customarily, one fisherman works the decoy, a painted wooden fish like object, tied to a line and a 'jig' stick. The decoy is weighted so that it will sink and has metal fins and a tail that can be bent so that it will move in large swooping circles when the stick is jigged. The other fisherman holds the spear and hopefully is smart enough to use it when the time comes.

Danny was just going home for lunch when we knocked on the door and he invited Bill and I to use the house until he returned. We agreed and took our respective positions around the hole sitting in the comfortably warm house with our skates on. This was my first experience fishing from a dark house, so Bill was instructing me and allowed me to hold the spear while he operated the decoy. It was fascinating, sitting in the comfortable dark and being able to clearly see the river bottom which was about ten feet underneath us. It was strangely quiet except for the occasional boom of the ice cracking as the river continued to freeze. We hadn't been there long and I was somewhat hypnotized watching the decoy quietly circle under the ice, when Bill whispered, "Here he comes!"

"Where?" says I, and as I uttered these words, into the hole, directly between my feet and about two feet under the ice, drifted a very large Northern Pike. I had never before experienced that which is commonly known as 'buck fever', but I was so stricken at that moment. The fish was so big and so close and I couldn't let go of the spear!

Bill was going nuts! "Spear it! Spear it!" he kept saying in a stage whisper as the fish swam out of sight.

Before Bill could begin berating me for my mental breakdown, he whispered again with not a little urgency in his voice, " Here he comes again!"

And once more the fish drifted into the hole and once again I was unable to release the spear, making just enough of a splash to frighten the fish. Chagrined, as the fish swam away, I handed the spear to Bill and predictably that was the last that we saw of that fish or any other that day. Needless to say, I was a laughing stock at school.

Yet another fish house story if I may; I worked for a few summers as a surveyors helper to the Hubbard County Surveyor. The last year, I worked for Bob McClelland, a former neighbor, a pilot and an all around good guy. He told me this story;

"One winter weekend, a friend of his (we'll call him Tom) had invited Bob to join him in his fish house on a remote lake quite a few miles form PR. So Bob fired up his monoplane already equipped with skis for the winter and flew out to the lake for an afternoon of fishing. Bob landed on the lake and taxied his aircraft toward Tom's fish house.

"Tom and his Labrador pup had been fishing quietly for

a few hours when they heard the hum of Bob's approaching airplane as he circled the lake. The sound became scarcely more than a whisper as he reduced power, made his approach, touched down and then taxied toward the fish house. As Tom opened the fish house door to welcome Bob, the pup looked out into the blinding sunlight and saw the approaching aircraft with its spinning propellor just a few yards from the door. At that moment, Bob gunned the engine to turn the ship around. These sudden combined sensations were too much for the pup who leaped into Tom's arms. Tom took a single, fateful step backwards and into the hole they both went.

"Bob helped the pup and Tom out of the frigid water and both soon dried off, thanks to the fish house stove. No real harm done. But, only Bob thought that the incident was funny."

OK, one more ice fishing story. Leech Lake is a large, beautiful lake about 30 miles east of Park Rapids. Citizens of the town of Walker are blessed to be able to live on the south shore of this scenic and wonderful lake. Leech Lake is also known for its population of Muskies or Muskelunge, a unique breed of large and predatory game fish. The lake is famous among the few hardy anglers who have the time and patience to pursue these crafty creatures. It is legal to take them with tackle (rods and reels for you neophytes) but it is illegal to spear them.

A distant relative of mine, one of the Sarff clan of ancestors had a fish house on Leech Lake. Young Sarff would spend nearly every afternoon after school during ice fishing season fishing for Northern Pike. One late afternoon as it was getting too dark to fish, Sarff had extinguished the fire in the stove and was putting his equipment away, preparatory to going home for supper when he saw a large 'something' drift into the hole just under the ice. Thinking that the 'something' was a log and would freeze into and foul the hole, the Sarff boy stood and vigorously jammed his spear into the log. At this moment, the 'log' came to life and proceeded to raise hell with Sarff clinging gamely onto the end of the violently thrashing spear handle. After much of this activity, young Sarff somehow managed to wrestle the fish out of the hole into the fish house where the contest continued. After a number of minutes and with major damage resulting to the sides of the fish house, the exhausted duo ended up lying on the ice outside the house.

The fish turned out to be a huge Muskie, 52 inches in length and weighing 52 pounds. Young Sarff received a fine for spearing the fish illegally; but some of the Walker citizens paid the fine and also had a taxidermist mount the fish. For years the monster could be seen in the Pure Oil Station then at the intersection of Highways 371 and 34 a few miles east of Walker. The property has changed ownership a number of time since then and I don't know where the fish is now. It may still be there, although I haven't seen it for many years.

It was May 1944, I believe, just before my cousin Leo went into the Navy, when my cousin Leo, Francis Connelly, our high school coach, and I went fishing on the river. Actually we went up the river about a mile and into Mud Lake just east of the Fish Hook . Mud Lake was a spawning area for black bass and therefore was closed to fishing of any kind at any time. Exercising some very flimsy logic as an excuse, "bass fishing season was not open yet". Two negatives make a positive, right? We entered Mud Lake and proceeded to fish. That incredible day spoiled fishing for me for years to come. The fishing was fabulous! We caught so many bass that we began to have contests to see who could catch the most fish on consecutive casts. I even caught two fish on the same cast.

The fish were going crazy, probably because it was in the heart of the spawning season. We threw every fish back except one that was badly hurt. What a day! Oh yes, we were right across the river from Cussie Smith's house. Cussie was the game warden.

There are other stories about the river that I could tell, but these few should demonstrate the importance of the Fish Hook River and surrounding lakes to me during my early life as well as to others who have had the privilege to grow up in Park Rapids.

Chapter VII

Of War and Wars

"In Flanders fields the poppies blow between the crosses row on row, that mark our place; and in the sky the larks, still bravely singing, fly scarce heard amid the guns below. We are the Dead. Short days ago we lived, felt dawn, saw sunset glow; loved, and were loved, and now we lie in Flanders fields..."

from The Rouge Bouquet by Major John McCrae,
May 3, 1915 from the Ypres Salient in Belgium

A number of wars have occurred during my lifetime: World War II, the Korean War, the Vietnam War, Desert Storm, not to mention Granada, Panama, Haiti, Somalia and Bosnia. More recently we have the Afghan War against the Taliban, and the Al Qaida Terrorists, and now the conflict within Iraq. I believe that history will show that these last two conflicts mark the beginning of what will be known as World War III. In point of fact, WWIII probably began in 1992 with the first attempt by Muslim radicals to bring down the twin towers of the World Trade Center. Some of these 'wars' were labeled 'police actions'. Some lasted only a few days, but wars they all were; Americans died in each one. And, I'm sure that there will be more, God forbid, before I leave this earth.

World War I, 'The Great War' or 'The War to End All Wars' ended ten years before I was born, yet that war, as well as previous wars, had a certain impact on my life. World War II had a tremendous impact on my formative years. Because, all through high school, my friends and I lived under the near certainty that we would serve our country immediately upon graduation. Many of us did, and many did not wait until graduation.

With today's lack of emphasis on history in our schools, I wonder how many readers of this tome know anything about WWII, much less of WWI, the Spanish American War, and the American Civil War. Yet, each of these wars is not that far removed from my lifetime, and hence from yours, also. Think about it.

For perspective, each of the Memorial Day Celebrations (it was called Decoration Day back then, May 31st then, now the last Monday in May) was held at the old Auditorium. (The old Auditorium was on the site of the not-so-recent addition to the National Guard Armory on Highway 71 across from the old high school.) At each of these celebrations back then, a veteran of the American Civil War would be helped to the stage and was greeted by standing applause. I've forgotten his name, but he was a drummer boy in the Union Forces in the War Between the States and very much alive in the 1930's. My Grandma Black was born during that war so, for me, there were real live linkages to that era when I was a boy.

There were also many World War I veterans in Park Rapids, some carrying war wounds such as missing limbs or with respiration problems from their exposure to mustard gas in the trenches. There were victims of 'shell shock' and all veterans carried memory scars from that horror of a war. Each year, again at the annual Decoration Day event, Coe Hamlin would mount the stage of the Auditorium in WWI uniform and recite that moving poem *The Rouge Bouquet* parts of which are quoted at the beginning and at the end of this chapter. My friend Bill's father fought in the trenches in that war, although he and others rarely spoke of it or of their experiences there. My dad served as a rifleman in the National Guard in Long Prairie at that time and his unit had been called up to go to France when the Armistice was signed, putting an end to the fighting.

Each year there was a parade ending with a memorial service at the Highway 34 Bridge across the Fish Hook River; complete with volleys fired by a rifle squad from Company L of the local National Guard, followed by the playing of Taps. One year I was privileged to play the 'echo' to Taps from the bushes at the east end of the bridge. Another year, Jack McMahon flew his Piper Cub low and slow over the bridge and dropped a wreath into the river honoring veterans of previous wars and battles. People were unashamedly patriotic then and for decades later as well. Thank God!

After the end of WWI, some of the former aviators from that war turned to barnstorming in an effort to preserve their love for flying and still eke out a living. Some of these barnstormers would fly into Park Rapids in the summer, either singly or in pairs. They would announce their arrival by flying low over town a number of times. We kids would immediately run across town to the grass field west of town that served as an airport then, where we would marvel at the airplanes and the men who flew them. These were lazy, but exciting summer days for us. And then began the conflict in Europe that rapidly developed into World War II. This war had a lasting effect on my life and on those of my friends. And for me, there began a terrible fascination with war, and that war in particular, that is still with me.

In the late 1930's, as Hitler's armies began their Blitzkrieg invasion of the Sudetenland, then Poland and Czechoslovakia and with Great Britain's attempt at appeasement followed shortly by their declaration of war against Germany and Italy, our lives changed forever. At first Mom worried that the United States would become involved and that my brother and my cousins would be called to serve in the defense of our country. She read the Minneapolis Star and listened to WCCO and WDAY every day as the U.S. became drawn inevitably into the conflict. However, she did not live to see the culmination of her worries.

In the early years of WWII the United States served as a supplier of arms to those countries who later became our allies. Some Americans enlisted in British and Canadian armed forces such as the RAF and RCAF. One of the fine athletes from Bemidji and from the University of Minnesota, Jack McCormick, joined the Royal Air Force and flew a Spitfire defending England from Hitler's Luftwaffe. This was the pivotal air war, called the Battle of Britain, during those early days of the war when England and France were on their heels and Hitler's victory seemed certain. This brief, unique and heroic air war is well described by Patrick Bishop on the front flap of his book *Fighter Boys: "For 123 days, while Hermann Goering sent wave after wave of Luftwaffe fighters to rain down fire on Britain, three thousand RAF airmen fought back with a ferocity and agility that stunned the world."* Their tenacity and subsequent victory discouraged Hitler to the point that he gave up his plans to invade Britain. At the close of this epic battle, Winston Churchill paid tribute to these nineteen and twenty year old pilots and their ground crews in his unforgettable speech to the House of Commons: *"...Never in the field of human conflict was so much owed by so many to so few..."*

The draft was instituted early in 1941 and the U.S. began its final preparations for war. One cold February day in 1941, Company L of the Park Rapids National Guard was mobilized and marched to the Great Northern Depot for transport to Camp Rucker in Alabama. I was one of the few who saw them off as they boarded the train at the depot on that bleak morning. Perhaps there had been a ceremony at the Armory; I can't remember. In any event, I took pictures of them with my little camera (that I got by sending in Wheaties box tops) as they marched to the train. That was the last that I saw of some of the men and older boys from the neighborhood.

My cousins and I were at Grandma's house in Park Rapids that Sunday afternoon when we first heard of the Japanese sneak attack on Pearl Harbor. None of us knew where Pearl Harbor was and did not begin to understand what that event would mean to us. The next day, we listened on the school's PA system to President Roosevelt and the Congress declare war on Japan, Germany and Italy, the Axis Powers. And so America went to war in earnest.

As Mom had feared, the family went to war also. Wen failed his draft physical so was exempt from service. But my cousins went. Bill Gadbaw, after helping to build the Alcan Highway to Alaska, served as ship's company on a troop transport and took part in many of the bloody island landings in the South Pacific. Ken Gadbow was an officer in the U.S. Navy serving as a pilot of a blimp in anti-submarine patrol. He later married Ann, a Navy nurse in the hospital where Ken ended up when he forgot to take his high blood pressure medication before a surprise physical. Leo Gadbaw served on a Navy destroyer in the Pacific as fire director of four 40mm antiaircraft guns, witnessed a number of Kamikazi attacks on his battle group during the last frantic days of the war. Ruby Gadbaw worked for a government intelligence activity in Arlington, Virginia and later married Harry Sartain, who served with Patton's Army in the North African, Sicilian and Italian campaigns.

One of my friends, Dickie Miller's father had been captain of Company L and had been transferred to Brainerd's tank company just prior to mobilization. Years later I heard that Major Miller had been captured in the fall of the Phillipines and was among the few survivors of the Bataan Death March. His oldest son, Tom Miller, was killed in Italy, and much later, I learned that my friend Dickie, a West Point graduate, had been killed in Vietnam as had Rick Agather, my high school friend.

There was a World War II Congressional Medal of Honor recipient from Park Rapids, who appeared at Bond Rallies swathed in splints and bandages. I believe that his name was Hawkes.

Small blue-edged flags with a blue star in the center, were displayed in the windows of those homes where fathers and/or sons had been called to serve. When the blue star was replaced by a gold one, it meant that the family had lost a loved one. Many homes displayed more than one flag. The war touched everyone.

For those of us still at home, there was gas rationing; which didn't bother us because we didn't have a car. To conserve gasoline, the speed limit in the United States was set at 35 miles per hour. There was sugar rationing; there were bond drives and rubber and paper drives. Citizens were urged to start and to grow a Victory Garden.

There was a local draft board that decided who would be called in the next draft to be inducted into the Army. While there were some who were never called there were many more who were called up and who went and served without complaint. There were even more who didn't wait to be called but enlisted rather than wait. I doubt that anyone really wanted to put their life in harms way, but they went anyway. If there were demonstrations against the war, such news never reached Park Rapids. I don't believe that there were any such. Young men were ready to put their lives on the line to protect our freedoms back then; much more so than now, I believe. However, the exemplary conduct of our 100% volunteer troops in Afghanistan and Iraq is causing me to reconsider that last statement.

In high school, boys in the advanced shop classes made beautiful wooden scale models of aircraft, of our enemies as well as of ours. (No kits back then.) These models were painted flat black and were used by the military to train soldiers and sailors in aircraft identification classes.

Our high school also had a Junior Guard Company made up of high school boys who were trained in close order drill and in the manual of arms in preparation for their almost certain induction into the Army after graduation. From this group, we older boys moved into the Minnesota State Guard that replaced Company L of the National Guard following their mobilization. We met in the Armory once a week for more training in marching and in rifle handling and in first aid. We also served as honor guards for military funerals at local churches and cemeteries.

One of our physical education instructors, Mr. Christianson, felt that it was his job to personally prepare us boys for the rigors of rapidly approaching entry into the military services. I doubt that even the Marines basic training was any more physically demanding than was Christy's Phy Ed class. He invented, or so he said, a game called 'casket ball' where a giant ball was placed at the center of the basketball court, sophomores at one end, juniors at the other with no regard for equality of numbers. At the sound of the whistle, the ball was to be advanced to the opponent's end of the court. That was the only rule. The game ended when the ball was so advanced. There were no time outs for injuries. One of my friends, Don Driscoll, broke his ankle during one of these games and was told by Christy to take ten laps around the gym to 'work it off'.

Another one of Christy's fun games was Fox and Hounds. One class, either the sophomores or juniors were designated as the 'foxes' and the other the 'hounds'. The foxes were given a ten-minute head start and they would take off for the woods along the river south of town. They would set an ambush for the soon-to-follow hounds. Again, there were no rules. Forget the two-mile run out and back; that was only incidental. Some of the interesting occurrences were: numerous dunkings in the river by both sides, falls from trees, fist fights, hog tying and at least once a bound student was left dangling from the hay mow of a barn near to the river. Actually, it was a good way to work off hostilities if you had a disagreement with someone on the opposite team. Surprisingly, there were no serious injuries from this 'game' although there was more than one upset mother. Also, we were probably not that pleasant to be close to in the classes following. And there was Christy's version of basketball where each player played with a boxing glove on one hand. 'Nuff said. Christy must have been a closet sadist.

Germany capitulated on May 8, 1945 and the war

finally ended on August 14, 1945 with the Japanese surrendering unconditionally following the U.S. dropping of atomic bombs on Hiroshima and Nagasaki. As horrible as these two events were, they saved hundreds of thousands if not millions of lives on both sides because the Japanese surrender prevented the inevitable U. S. invasion of the Japanese mainland which the Japanese had pledged to defend to the last man, woman and child.

The war was finally over and the United States had prevailed! That evening, August 14th, when the news of the Japanese surrender reached Park Rapids, Main Street quickly filled with celebrators. Both fire trucks traveled up and down the street with sirens at full cry. Residents, including me, climbed aboard the trucks for a few transits up and down the street filled with cheering people. Truly a memorable night!

When the time came for us seniors to graduate, the draft was still on even though the fighting had ceased in both European and Pacific Theaters. Faced with the draft, we group of friends decided to join the Navy. We traveled together to Minneapolis by train for physicals and for indoctrination. Bill Skelton and Bill Lehnherr failed the Navy's eye examinations so they joined the Army. Bill Skelton served with an engineering battalion near the 'parallel' in Korea and watched the Chinese Communists prepare for war on their side of the line. Bill Lehnherr served in Korea as well, before and during the subsequent conflict. Duane Henry, star miler and captain of our track team had undergone an appendectomy six weeks earlier and was rejected by the Navy. So Duane went across the street and was accepted by the paratroopers and served with the 82nd Airborne.

So Chuck Williams, Lowell Mason and I joined the Navy and traveled by train to Minneapolis. After being cordially invited to "…please line up gentlemen to be sworn in…" we were then advised, "…OK you guys, you're in the Navy now! Now grab a broom and sweep down this #@&%* deck." But that's the beginning of another story. Suffice it to say, we learned a lot in the months that followed, grew up a little, and saw parts of the world that we had never seen and that most of us have not seen since. But, most importantly, for me, was that we qualified for the GI Bill of Rights which paid for over two years of my college. I doubt that many of us, and I know that I could not have afforded to go to college had it not been for Uncle Sam's largess.

The Korean and Vietnamese conflicts followed on the heels of WWII and had an immense impact on the country: divisiveness, much of which still remains. For the first time in our history, the United States had lost wars, two in a row and in each case to third world countries. We lost friends in both conflicts. And we learned, I hope, that if a war is to be fought, it should be fought to be won and it should be fought by professionals, not by politicians!

Now, in 2007, it appears that these lessons were not learned as the new Democrat controlled Congress broadcasts their intentions to cut and run from Iraq abandoning our troops as well as the Iraqi people. Does this promised action portend Iranian occupation of Iraq as soon as our troops leave? Will there be monumental civilian casualties and atrocities as happened immediately following our pull out from Viet Nam? I'm afraid that such terrible events are inevitable if we elect to leave before the job is completed. Once again, the once mighty U.S. will be defeated by a third world country. Will this ever end?

Perhaps the U.S. was too exhausted from the sacrifices of the 1940s and was unwilling to be drawn into another emotional turmoil. For whatever reason, I believe that my generation abdicated its duty to stand up for our freedoms and consequently we gave free reign to the free-love generation of the '60s and to the politically correctness gurus of the '90s. We have lost many, many of our freedoms during my lifetime. Now it remains for another generation to pick up these banners before our freedoms are gone altogether. I hope that it's not too late.

As I rewrite this chapter early in 2007, our country and our allies are fighting a worldwide war with the terrorists who brought down the World Trade Center Towers and attacked the Pentagon all on September 11, 2001. Although our troops are fighting and dying in Iraq and Afghanistan, there are terrorist attacks in other countries around the globe including the United States homeland. There are attacks against trains and refineries and we fear of a large attack somewhere in the U.S. at any time. There are strong indications that the backbone of the resistance in Iraq is provided not by Iraqis but by insurgent fighters from Iran and Syria and perhaps from other Arab countries as well. Finances for these outside excursions are being furnished by Iran, Syria and perhaps even by our 'friends' in Saudia Arabia. There is evidence that France, Germany and Russia have and are profiting by previous deals with Saddam Hussein and even high officials in the United Nations have apparently participated in kick backs from the Oil For Food Program. Liberals within the Democrat Party have developed a virulent hatred for President Bush. They did everything in their power to prevent his reelection in 2004. "Anyone But Bush" was their unofficial campaign slogan. Thankfully, George W. prevailed easily in the election and the country has four more years, at this writing, to strengthen our security and to rally our people and our allies in the war against terror.

This is the climate for what is probably the early years

of World War III. This war is rapidly becoming a war of radical Muslim fundamentalist fanatics against America and Christianity and Judaism and is being fought all over the world. No matter who wins the next U.S. election, this war will go on for many years and will be fought inside many countries. I believe that there will be many casualties within American cities as well as cities in other countries. These terrorists are without consciences and cannot be trusted or cannot be negotiated with. The only way that the United States will emerge victorious from this conflict is to confront and defeat the enemy on each and every front. Anything less will only prolong the war and could eventually result in the defeat of our civilization as we know it today. Do I sound pessimistic? I am! Is the situation serious? It most certainly is!

And there are other threats from within the United States. Federal Judges have ruled that the words "under God" cannot be uttered in the Pledge of Allegiance, that it is unconstitutional to do so. They are inclined to legislate from the bench without regard for the Constitution. The Hollywood elite denigrate their privileged life in America, and some members of Congress criticize and divide the country instead of leading. Consequently, I feel compelled to do a little preaching. Are you ready?

We, you and I and many others, are privileged to live in the greatest country on Earth. There are those who disagree with this statement and who are trying in many different ways to tear our country down, to bend and even abolish our constitution. They hold up the governments of other countries as examples that we should follow in the U.S. Some even advocate abdication of our laws and freedoms to the 'magnanimous and unbiased wisdom' of the United Nations. God help us! To these vocal few, I say, "Please choose a country more to your liking and quietly leave us and go and live there. But, leave us alone!"

I am tired of the drumbeat for 'global warming'. I am infuriated by the government sponsored expenditure of millions and probably billions of dollars to "protect" mice and insects and minnows whose existence may or may not be threatened. I will always believe that the health and welfare of people takes precedence over that of bugs, plants and rodents. Nor do I subscribe to the myth that we puny humans can exert more influence on the climate than can the sun and the oceans and the earth itself. Environmentalists are really giving our environment a bad name!

Every time I pass through an airport, which is no more frequently than absolutely necessary, I can't help but count up the millions of lost hours of productivity each day caused by the futile and ineffective, I believe, efforts to "protect" the flying public from terrorists and terrorism. There must be a better way. I have always loved to fly and I still do. But I hate today's airports and I just don't fit into the cramped seats that are standard in the steerage sections of airliners today. Rude, inconsiderate travelers make this confinement even more unbearable. Consequently, I fly only when absolutely necessary and then reluctantly.

The good ol' US of A was conceived and built by men who put their very lives and fortunes and the lives of their families on the line in order to stand up for their beliefs. Men like Adams and Jefferson and Washington, and indeed every signer of the Declaration of Independence literally risked their lives and all of their properties in order to advance the cause of Freedom. Many did pay with their lives and with their worldly possessions in the conflict with England.

Today, we who believe in our country and value our freedoms are yet loath to risk facing the sharp tongues and criticisms of the vocal few who, for whatever reason and in the name of political correctness, try to change our Constitution to accommodate their desires of the moment and to whittle away at our remaining freedoms. At some point, and probably in the not-too-distant future, we will have to take a stand. Without fear, we will have to make ourselves and our opinions known to the detractors of our freedoms and of the United States. There are those within our borders and, God help us, within our very government, as well as those outside our borders who would like to see the end of America as we know it. We must not let this happen!

For those who say that there is no place for God in our country, let us examine some of our history. And for those who have not had the privilege of learning some of this history during your school years, let me recommend the following evidence that God is indeed interested in preserving the United States as an entity in this world:

In 1776, at the beginning of United States history, there seemed to be no possible way that George Washington's rag-tag, ill equipped, poorly trained army could prevail against the world's most powerful army at the zenith of Great Britain's power. But they did! God's will? I think so.

Nearly a century later, the Confederate Army was having its way against a larger, better equipped Union Army. Yet at Gettysburg in Pennsylvania, Colonel Joshua Chamberlain refused to allow the Southern Forces to turn his flank at Little Round Top on July 2nd. And the next day, the South's brilliant general, Robert E. Lee made the fatal error of ignoring General Longstreet's pleas and instead sent Pickett's Division on its ill-fated charge across two miles of open field, in closely ordered ranks, marching into the muzzles of Union cannon. Haven't heard of these events? Rent the video *Gettysburg* or read the historically accurate novel *Killer Angels* by Michael Shaara. Or better still, visit the battlefield at Gettysburg and stand behind that low stone wall where the Union troops lay waiting and imagine the long, gray rows of Confederate soldiers as they emerged from the forest and formed into orderly ranks. Visualize them marching, not running or charging, but marching across that field as Yankee cannon took an ever increasing toll on the diminishing ranks of the stubborn and disciplined rebel soldiers. If you can do this and come away with dry eyes, you're a better person than I am. The courage of those men who fought there, those who lived and those who died, is unimaginable to me. Yet that courage was typical of those who built and fought for this country. And, I believe, that God had a hand in the crucial events that decided the outcome of that battle, that turning point of the American Civil War and the preservation of the Union.

For another real example, consider the Battle of Midway early in World War II. The US Navy was all but destroyed by the Japanese at Pearl Harbor. However, the Navy's carrier force had put out to sea only days before the attack. Did God have a hand in the decision to get the aircraft carriers out of harms way? Maybe. Then the Japanese sent their own carrier centered strike force against the tiny US base on Midway Island with the plan to invade the Aleutian Islands, stepping stones to Alaska and perhaps to the mainland of the U.S. The patched up survivors of Pearl Harbor and the subsequent Battle of the Coral Sea tried valiantly to thwart this attack. When they finally located the Japanese Strike Force, US navy air attacks were completely ineffective. Torpedo Squadron 8 was wiped out with only one survivor and didn't make a single hit on a Japanese ship. Yet even as the battle seemed to be lost, US Navy dive bombers were again able to locate the Japanese fleet. At this moment, the Japanese fighter cover had landed on the decks of the carriers for refueling and their strike aircraft were on the decks changing munitions from bombs to torpedoes. Relatively unopposed, the Navy dive bombers struck. Within minutes, literally, four of the five Japanese carriers had been sunk and the Battle of Midway was over. The United States Navy had snatched victory out of the jaws of defeat. Luck? Coincidence? Maybe. Divine intervention? I like to think so. Want to learn more? Read the book *Midway* or rent the video of the same name; the historic events portrayed are real and accurate. Or better still, find a veteran of that battle if you can, buy him a cup of coffee and listen to what he has to say.

Why did Hitler refuse to exercise his advantage over the British after France had fallen and after the humiliating but successful evacuation of British troops at Dunkirk? Why did he not attack the reeling English on their own soil? How were the out numbered Royal Air Force Spitfires and Hurricanes able to defeat the German Luftwaffe at the crucial Battle of Britain? How were the American, Canadian and British forces able to cling to their few yards of beach at Normandy and indeed advance over the cliffs in the face of German fire from defensive positions that had been designed and constructed to defeat just such an invasion? Why did Rommel fall for the Allied ruse and send his tanks to Calais instead of to Normandy? How were the US Marines able to take Tarawa and Guadalcanal while suffering terrible losses on the beaches of those tiny islands? How could they dislodge the Japanese from their tunnels and caverns in their suicidal defense of Iwo Jima and Okinawa? Why was the United States able to win the race with Germany to develop the first atomic weapons and to use them to end the war before the pending invasion of the Japanese mainland? The Japanese would have defended their homeland to the last causing unimaginable casualties on both sides. And do you not think that Hitler would have used atomic weapons against us had he won that race?

I tend not to believe in or put much faith in coincidence. I believe that a Supreme Being had a hand, and an interest, in determining the outcome of most if not all of these events. May God continue to be on our side in the coming years and decades. I think that we're going to need all of His Help that we can get. God Bless and Help America!

"...Take up the quarrel with the foe: to you with failing hands we throw the torch; be yours to hold it high. If ye break faith with us who die, we shall not sleep, though poppies grow in Flanders fields."

From The Rouge Bouquet by Major John McCrae

Chapter VIII

PRHS

Pile the score in a stack for the Orange and the Black...and Park Rapids goes zipping along...
from PRHS School Song – author unknown

My graduating class of 1946 was the first class to occupy the "new school building" from 7th through 12th grades. We felt privileged to have such a new modern school for our classes, especially after we had to travel all over Park Rapids, to various community buildings in order to finish grades 5 through 6. Under the tutelage of Miss Knudsen, Mrs. Johnston and Miss Jones, my Junior High years passed quickly and relatively uneventfully. One morning in early December, 1941 we sat in class and listened to then President Franklin Delano Roosevelt deliver his famous *"...a date that will live in infamy..."* speech as Congress declared war on Germany, Japan and

Italy. Little did we know then the import and the impact of that speech and the events that followed.

And, one Fall morning a deer jumped through an eighth grade window about an hour before classes started; so no harm done, except for the window that is.

Junior high marked my introduction to intramural basketball. I was made a member of the Bears, a team coached by Donnie Hinckley, one of the stars of the varsity basketball team. Unlike 7th and 8th grade boys today, I was completely clueless regarding basketball fundamentals. I had a vague understanding of the rules, but I couldn't dribble, I couldn't shoot, and I certainly didn't understand defense. And I was about 5' 10" tall and skinny. As a result, my friends would come to our practices and games, mostly to laugh at me and to make fun of my ungainly attempts to master the sport that would later become so important to me. The most positive aspect of my early basketball experience was that we had to shower after every practice and every game. This was the first time that my archaic hygiene had been exposed to showers and on a nearly daily basis. The results were dramatic and much appreciated, I'm sure, by my close friends and relatives.

There were so few boys in my class and especially those who were interested in athletics, that I became a starter on the varsity (we called it the 'first team') when I became a high school freshman. My first competitive game was against Bemidji High School, played on the Bemidji State Teachers College floor. There were only two boys on our team who had ever played in a 'real' basketball game before that night. I don't believe that I even touched the ball in that game. We lost 52 to 12 and I think that Johnny Fraser scored all of our 12 points. We may have won a few games that year, but I don't remember if there were any other schools whose teams were sufficiently inept to become our victims. I know that there weren't many.

I didn't go out for any other sports that year. Wen got me a job at Bishops Clothing Store starting in March, so I couldn't try out for the track team. And Eula wouldn't let me play football, which was a good thing because I would surely have been severely injured if not mortally wounded. A physical specimen I was not. At 6'1" and 130 pounds my freshman year, all I had going for me was an advanced case of 'tall and skinny'.

But there were some memorable events my Freshman year in high school. The first was Freshman Initiation Day. This was a traditional annual event when on some undisclosed day early every Fall, freshman, on their way to school, were ambushed by upperclassmen (we didn't know about 'upper class persons' back then) who then painted the freshman's faces using various colors of chalk. The event was generally painless and aside from some embarrassment, was harmless. "Just wait until next year when we get our turn!"

The really formative event that I shall never forget was my election as Freshman Class President. This was a complete surprise, because we didn't have a campaign, in fact the election itself was unanticipated to most of us. I believe that our principal, Miss Vida Mae Lewis, was responsible. Our entire class was assembled in the cafeteria. Miss Lewis called for nominations for the various class offices. There were no nominations for president, so Miss Lewis nominated me and had me stand on one of the cafeteria tables so everyone could see me. I was reluctant to stand on the table because my shoes had been recently half-soled and there were nails protruding from the soles; I was afraid that they would scratch the table. Never the less, I stood on the table in front of my new classmates and since there were no other nominations, I won by a landslide. As president-elect I was then responsible for conducting the remainder of the election and the meeting. I was clueless as usual, so Miss Lewis kindly walked me through Robert's Rules of Order in real time, and I thus became familiar with how to run a meeting without getting into too much trouble.

I went out for track my sophomore year and then for football my junior year, continuing with basketball, band and choir, although this was the year that my voice started to change. Our basketball team won a few more games each year, as did the football team. Our track team was always good, winning the District 29 meet nearly every year and generally the Region 8 meet as well. I qualified for state my junior year in the high jump and pole vault and went to the State Meet by myself. I did poorly, not qualifying in either event.

I'll always remember my first football game; it was my junior year and at Fergus Falls. I didn't start but played most of the game at right end. My opponent across the line was Mark Foss who started and starred at the University of North Dakota the following year. He greeted my arrival in the first half with *"OK let's get the new guy."* Thus encouraged, I proceeded to make tackle after tackle. This was not difficult since they ran nearly every play over my position. They continued to run at me because they gained yardage nearly every play. I don't remember the final score, but we got beat, bad. Boy, did I have a headache after that game! But we repaid the favor the next year.

Our team improved with every game my junior year and actually won a few games. One interesting home-and-home series was with Walker. Walker only played eight-man football and we played eleven-man. So when we played Walker, we would play eight-man for the first half and eleven-man the second half. We won both ways. Walker had a big jovial guy named Teenus Carlson. Teenus played fullback on offense and linebacker on defense. Everyone went both ways in those days. Anyway, Teenus and I became pretty good friends, and he went on to play at the University of Minnesota the next year. In fact, he played in the first university game that I ever saw. He threw snowballs at the other guys during warm-ups.

We played Wadena for Homecoming that year. Wadena had a pretty good team. They scored first but failed to convert, leading 6 to 0 late in the game. With Wadena punting from deep in their own territory, Chuck Hinckley, our right tackle, blew in and blocked the punt. The ball was bouncing crazily toward their goal line. In those few seconds, as I approached the ball, I was trying to decide whether to try to pick it up and run, risking a fumble or to play it safe and fall on it. Hearing a thunder of footsteps behind me, I decided on the latter approach and fell on it. That's the good news. The bad news was that the thunder of footsteps belonged to my guys. Had I picked the ball up and run, I would have scored easily and we would have won. As it was, we failed to score on that possession and lost 6 to 0. I'll certainly never forget that game.

Our football coach that year was Francis Connelly, a graduate of Bemidji State Teachers College. His assistant was a mountain of a man named Bud Boeringer. Bud had played center for Notre Dame under Knute Rockne and with the famed Four Horsemen and the Seven Mules. Bud had been head coach at the University of Detroit until they dropped football during the war. He had a summer home on one of the lakes around PR and agreed to help coach for a few years. He introduced the Notre Dame Box formation to our team which turned out to be quite successful for us. In addition to being a good coach, Bud was also a very nice guy…..and colorful. When Bob McFarren broke his nose in the Sebeka game, Bob ran to Bud crying: *"Is it broken? Is it broken?"*

Carefully examining Bob's nose that was now about an inch removed from its normal position and shifting his ever-present chew to the other side of his mouth, Bud replied, *"Naw it ain't broke, but you sure bent the hell out of it!"*

Our basketball team won about half of our games my junior year. The game of note was against Bemidji on our floor, just a few weeks before the tournaments. We somehow took Bemidji into overtime! A matter of pride even though we lost in O.T. and lost to them again in the tournament. That year, Bemidji went to the State tournament and was Consolation Champion after losing to Minneapolis Patrick Henry in the opener. Patrick Henry had 6' 10" Jim McIntyre at center, who went on to become an All-American at Minnesota. Bemidji's center was Dick Lawrence, about 6' 2" tall, a part Indian kid from Red Lake. Dick held McIntyre to the lowest score of the tournament and went on to become the only freshman at U of M ever to letter in three sports: football, basketball and baseball. A good guy and a fine athlete.

During my senior year, PRHS athletics reached its zenith, for me at least. We lost our opening football game at Bemidji, badly as usual. There were two aspects of that game that were memorable. The first but least important was that, after many, many years, the old orange and black jerseys and torn and patched canvas pants that Panther players had worn for years, were finally retired in favor of new white jerseys and khaki colored pants . We still had our old black molded leather helmets without face masks. (Hadn't been invented yet.) Resplendent in our new uniforms we went on to lose 7 – 34. The really sad note that night was that Dick Mack, my friend who should have started at right end, but instead followed me up and down the sidelines, shouting encouragement, was fatally injured in an automobile accident on the way home after the game. Dick died a few days later, and his teammates were pall bearers at his funeral.

We won the next game and then lost the third game at Aitken's homecoming, 12 – 7 in the final moments. Those were the last touchdowns scored against us that year. In fact there were only two more points scored against us the rest of the season. In the next game at Wadena, Dick Webb centered the ball over Bennie Noland's head and into the end zone for a safety. We won big in that game and then shut out our next four opponents, repaying Fergus Falls for the indignity suffered the previous year by beating them 27 – 0 on our field on a snowy day. That was a cold day and we all dressed for the cold. I was wearing a pair of long underwear pants under my pads. These were war times, remember, and elastic was hard to find. My long handles had no elastic but did have a button. On the opening kickoff, I threw a block and popped that button. My long johns then slipped down far enough to make it difficult to run. For the rest of the game, after nearly every play, I had to pause and pull my underwear up. Embarrassing!

We finished the season at 6 and 2 and started an undefeated streak that lasted for 25 consecutive games, a record that may still be unbroken in Minnesota High School football.

Our good fortunes extended into basketball when we posted a 24 to 4 won/lost record. Once again we lost to Bemidji in the district tournament even though we beat the Bemidji College freshman three times and these same college freshman beat the Bemidji Lumberjacks every time that they played them Were we jinxed? I think so.

Track was always my favorite sport. Maybe it was because Track and Spring always happened at the same time. Maybe it was because I participated in the field events so that we were able to lounge in the sun on the fresh grass while we waited our turn to jump or vault or whatever. Those were halcyon days.

There were huge differences in the events that I participated in back then compared to present days versions. Pole vaulters today use fiberglass poles that flex and launch the vaulter to stratospheric heights. And these pampered athletes land on their backs on thick air cushioned pads that look like they would be fun to sleep on. We used bamboo poles that sometimes broke or splintered at the most inopportune times. Watch out for those splinters! Later on in college we used aluminum and tapered Swedish steel poles, but I always preferred bamboo.

Did we land on air filled mattresses? Oh no! Far from it. We jumped into pits filled with sawdust or shavings: and at the St. Johns Invitational, filled with sand. Since it would have been suicidal to land on your back in those pits, our style required that we pole vaulters land feet first and roll to prevent injury.

The same was true for the high jump: sawdust or shavings and sand in the pit. Not surprisingly the Fosberry Flop was not invented until years later when it was preceded by introduction of those wonderful blue, air-filled pads. Track must truly be a wonderful sport today.

In spite of these hardships, I qualified for state in four events, high jump, pole vault, broad jump and high hurdles. I participated in only two of those events and tied for second in the high jump and for third in the pole vault with a borrowed pole. After the meet, Jim Kelly, U of M Track Coach asked me to look him up after I got out of the Navy, an incident that I completely forgot about until many years later. I wonder how my life might have been changed had I remembered and had contacted him.

Did I mention how I learned to pole vault? I thought not. When I was 11 or 12 years old and living at Dutton's, Wen cut a pine pole about eight feet long and tied a clothes line between two trees for a cross bar. There was a knot on that pole that rubbed my chest raw and occasionally straddling the clothes line was an unanticipated thrill. But I learned the fundamentals never the less. Later, I watched the 'big guys' as they worked out at the Park: Charlie Lord, Frankie McNulty, and Vern Shuckhart, soon to be Dr. Vernon Shuckhart, DDS. They sometimes let me vault with them and gave me pointers.

I mentioned in preceding paragraphs the differences between the equipment and facilities that we tracksters enjoyed back then compared to those used by track athletes today. There were significant differences in other sports as well.

Our basketball trunks (pants for you folks in Rio Linda) didn't even extend to mid-thigh let alone to below the knee baggies as worn by present day hoopsters. And, we only had one set of uniforms that we wore both at home as well as on the road. Two handed shots were *de rigueur* for free throws as well as for field goals. I was severely reprimanded by my coach when I jumped and shot the ball from over my head. "Edam," he shouted, "you wouldn't try to shoot a rifle from over your head would you?"

No face masks or cages graced the front of our football helmets which were made of molded leather with a small amount of rubber padding inside. The shock of blows to our heads were attenuated somewhat by these helmets, but it was not uncommon for the wearer to lose consciousness briefly after such an onslaught. Facial injuries such as broken noses, fat lips, lost teeth (although we did wear mouth guards), abrasions and lacerations were also not uncommon. On the other hand, our equipment limitations required different techniques. We employed shoulder blocks and cross-body blocks which probably reduced neck and back injuries that seem to be more prevalent today.

I've devoted most of this chapter to athletics in high school because they were very important to me. Academically, I was not a bad student, graduating 3rd in a class of 44. Betty Bakken was Valdectorian and Betty Condiff was Salutatorian. We only had 14 boys in our class, a ratio of almost 3 to 1; but that is a whole 'nuther story.

There was an incident my last year of high school that still bothers me; I think of it from time to time and still wonder if I did the right thing. Both Mr. Mevig, our superintendent, and Miss Lewis, our principal, were removed by the school board in midyear, to be effective at the end of the school year. These two administrators had been at PRHS for many years and were loved by all, with the exception of the school board apparently. The student body was up in arms at the announcement and as president of the senior class, I felt that we had to do something about this travesty. Meeting with others in the class, we decided to call a student body protest strike for one day complete with a parade down Main Street. So a date was set and a strike vote was called for. The vote was held and Miss Lewis and I retired to her office to count the votes minutes after the ballots were collected from each room. Overwhelmingly, the wish of the student body was to strike. When the results became obvious, Miss Lewis asked me to go on the school's PA system and to tell the students that the vote was negative: not to strike. We discussed the issue for some time and she was adamant that a strike would do more harm than good and that it was an action not favored by either her or Mr. Mevig. So I did as she requested; I went on the PA system and announced that the vote was against a strike and that the subject was closed. And so it was. There was no demonstration of any kind, and Miss Lewis and Mr. Mevig left the school quietly at the end of the term. Miss Lewis worked at the Hubbard County Court House for a few years, and then disappeared. I saw Mr. Mevig briefly on Main Street after I returned from Boot Camp at Great Lakes; then he too disappeared.

Did I do right by lying to the student body about the strike vote and going against their wishes? I'll never know; but it has bothered me ever since. To those classmates of mine in 1946 who may read this now, I hope that you will understand and forgive me for my perfidy.

This is a good time to list those people in high school who influenced my life in later years. Miss Vida Mae Lewis would have to be first on the list for many reasons. She taught me to love American history which evolved into a love of all kinds of history that influences my life today. (Can you tell that from the contents of this book so far?) And, I have always felt that she understood me better than anyone of the other faculty at PRHS. She didn't put up with any of my nonsense, yet she was kind and fair; a truly great lady and I regret any grief that my immature shenanigans may have caused her.

Miss Lucy Jensen taught me the wonders of mathematics, geometry and algebra and introduced me to trigonometry. The strong base that she gave to me in these subjects allowed me to pursue engineering as a profession and left me with an appreciation and an interest in numbers that exists today. In spite of this background, I have great difficulty in understanding these subjects as taught in today's schools by today's teachers. It's mostly a matter of nomenclature, I think. But to my grandchildren: don't ask me to help you with your math homework. I'll probably get the right answers, but your teacher won't like my methods.

Mr. Harold Johnson, Physics Teacher, taught the subject well, but most importantly encouraged me and Mase and Chuck Williams to take the Eddy Test prior to enlisting in the Navy. He tutored us in basic electronics so that we were subsequently able to pass the test and be assured of acceptance into the Navy's Electronics School before even being sworn in. We also enlisted as Seamen First Class and became Petty Officers 3rd Class upon graduation.

Mr. Quentin Jones was our Scoutmaster and Track Coach. He was a soft spoken man who led by example and by encouragement. I don't think that I ever heard a negative comment from this man. He encouraged me to take Junior Life Saving instruction which allowed me to become a life guard and swimming and life saving instructor. "Squinty", as we called him, was solely responsible for the excellent track program at PRHS. He sometimes called me "Wendy" because he had been Wen's teacher as well. He left during my early years in high school for a better job, I suppose, in Thief River Falls.

Mr. Earl Turnblad, our band director and civics teacher, may not have been the greatest teacher in the world, but he was a fine man and the best cornet player that I encountered for many years. He had served in WWI and brought a charming French lady home as his wife. He allowed me to play in the high school band from when I was in fourth grade until he left Park Rapids.

High school had a profound effect on my life, mostly good, but there were some negatives as well, of course. I probably spend too much time reveling in the positive experiences and ruminating about the negatives. Those days are gone forever; only memories, pride and some regrets remain.

PRHS Panthers 1945

Panthers Basketball

Chapter IX

Anchors Aweigh

"God our Father, strong to save ,whose arm doth bind the restless wave and bids the mighty ocean deep, its own appointed limits keep...Hear us as we rise to thee, for those in peril on the sea."

from The Navy Hymn

It was only a few weeks between high school and the Navy, yet it could have been a lifetime in terms of how my life changed in such a short time. In a previous chapter, I related how my classmates and I had decided to enlist in the Navy rather than be drafted into the Army even though WWII had already come to an end. Now having been sworn in Minneapolis, I was bound for boot camp. My solo train trip from Minneapolis to Great Lakes Naval Training Station marked only the second time that I had ever been outside of Minnesota. I arrived at the main gate at Great

Lakes late at night and was directed to my temporary barracks to await the formation of my boot company. During this first week, I wore civvies, walked around the base, played in pick-up basketball games (where my watch that Eula had given to me for graduation was stolen, when the guy who volunteered to hold the watches quietly left with all of them), and went to church at the Mainside Chapel that first Sunday. This church service was made memorable when the Great Lakes Blue Jacket Choir sang *Balm in Gilead* with a young tenor with the voice of an angel singing the solo.

But all good things must come to an end. The next day we were summoned to a large bare room where we were each assigned to a small painted square on the floor of this building. There we were given a cardboard box and instructed to put all, all, of our clothing into this box which was subsequently shipped to our respective home addresses. Standing in that small square, stark naked, waiting for the next event in our now uncertain young lives was one of the loneliest moments of my life until then. We didn't have to wait long.

We were measured, and had Merthiolate numbers painted on our bare bodies and we began a circuitous parade through an adjacent room. As we rounded each corner in this nude parade we were shot here with this needle, and there with another needle as we turned the next corner. We were commanded to bend over, to do this and to do that; each maneuver was a new indignity. Finally when our naked, vulnerable bodies had been sufficiently painted, penetrated and otherwise violated we entered another room where each us was handed a mattress cover, euphemistically known as a fart sack, and instructed how to hold this container just so. As we progressed through this room, a line of sadistic young 'Boots' dispensed our new

Navy wardrobe, everything from brogans to underwear by bouncing each item off of our unprotected faces and into our fart sacks. Not to worry, our turn to practice this sadism would come within the following weeks as we too entered "work week".

Sufficiently supplied with our new threads, we retired to another room where a petty officer, completely unsympathetic to questions, allowed us to try on certain items of clothing and instructed us how to pack our sea bags. We proceeded to a "barber shop" where a number of civilian "barbers" competed to see which one could create the most ridiculous haircut in the shortest time. I escaped relatively unharmed and silently gave thanks that I had seen fit to leave home with my standard jock's crew cut. We were then informed that we were members of Boot Company 220, were formed into a ragged formation and marched a few dusty miles to Camp Green Bay, a misnomer if there ever was one. There we were assigned to a second story barracks filled with steel double bunks in an aged two story frame building that would be our home for the next eight weeks. There we became acquainted with Chief Petty Officer Skiftness who would be our chief tormentor for our time in beautiful Camp Green Bay. The epitome of grace and breeding, our chief greeted us with, "Get off those @#$%&* bunks and stand at attention! Your heart may belong to momma but from now on, your ass belongs to me!" And so it was!

Taps was at 2100 (Navy time term) and that first night, we were allowed to sleep until 0200 (another Navy time term very early in the morning actually) when we were aroused from our dreamless sleep to do laundry. No matter that there was not room in the laundry for all of us. Chow was at 0600, and then began our metamorphosis from civilians into sailors of the United States Navy. We learned to march. (I thought that the Army marched and that the Navy rode around in nice ships.) But we marched, and marched and marched. Those who were unable to grasp the rudiments of close order drill were provided with a bucket placed over their heads and commanded to shout "I am a knucklehead!" over and over again. This did not noticeably improve their marching techniques until much later. Again, I was extremely grateful for the Junior ROTC experience in high school that enabled me to survive this part of our training.

Meals were served in an "H" shaped building with four chow halls connected by a central scullery. We paraded along the serving line where comedian wannabees dispensed our daily sustenance with such witticisms as "Do you like buttermilk sailor?" followed by raucous laughter as he splashes a pat of butter into my milk cup.

Following consumption of our meal we would proceed to the scullery where we would dispose of uneaten food (there was grief given out if we threw away too much food even if it was inedible) and then put dishes and trays into racks for washing. As we left the scullery, the denizens of that operation would shout "Don't let that door slam sailor!" Out of reflex, we would put our hands out to catch the screen door. We hadn't had time to realize that the screen door was covered by an electric fly screen. More raucous laughter as we inspected the cross hatched pattern burned into the palms of our hands.

Since we had been good little Boots, we were allowed to sleep until 0400 the next morning. That ungodly hour became the time for the start of each day for most of our remaining time in Boot Camp. So we endured with seven hours of sleep each night. Seems like enough doesn't it. But please don't overlook watch duty. Each of us was assigned to watch duty as dictated by the Watch List that was posted each day. Each watch lasted four hours and could occur any time between 1600 and 0800. Watches would encompass such duties as: Fire Watch, Bell Watch, Security Watch, Boiler Room Watch, etc. Some of these duties such as Boiler Room Watch were quite casual, where we could wear dungarees and could sit down during the watch. Others, such as Bell Watch, were formal. There we wore dress blues, carried a rifle and marched back and forth along a designated path and rang the bell according to Navy protocol on each half hour observing Navy formalities throughout the watch. One morning, I was assigned the 0400 to 0600 watch in the Chief Petty Officers Quarters. One of my jobs was to make morning coffee. Fortunately, I was relieved before anyone tasted what I hoped would pass for coffee.

As a result, we were always tired. There were times when we actually slept while standing, if time permitted.

In spite of all this, we gradually became sailors. We learned rifle drill and could field strip and reassemble the Garand M1 rifle in less than a minute, blindfolded. We fired the M1 on the rifle range, and the Colt .45 in the indoor range. We learned to fight oil fires. We learned how to stand shipboard watches properly and to identify friendly and enemy aircraft and ships. We learned how to handle lines and to tie various kinds of knots. We learned how to handle small boats, and of course, we learned military courtesy and discipline. We watched movies on hygiene and the hazards of promiscuous and unprotected sex. And thus prepared, we were given two weeks leave and returned home after which we were turned loose on the greater Navy and various parts of an unsuspecting world.

Returning from leave, and after a two weeks stint in the Outgoing Units Barracks, a lovely barracks room the size of a basketball court, filled with three-tier bunks, a room where the lights were rarely extinguished, where men were coming and going all night, I finally started Basic Electronics Technicians school.

To my everlasting shame, I nearly flunked out of this school. This was because I began these classes as though I were in still high school. As in high school, I rarely studied, I went to base movies frequently, I sang in the Great Lakes Glee Club and played on the Great Lakes Basketball Team. These were fun activities but I should have paid more attention to my studies and to my homework.

On most Sunday afternoons that Fall, the Glee Club sang a half-hour concert over WGN Chicago Radio. During the Christmas Holidays, after our afternoon concert, our group reconvened on Michigan Avenue in front of the Wrigley Building and serenaded passers-by with Christmas carols while we waited for our bus. There were large flakes of snow falling and we made quite a picture, a picture that appeared in the *Chicago Tribune.* This festive event nearly ended in disaster, however. Our Navy bus driver finally arrived to take us back to Great Lakes after spending his time, apparently, in one or more bars in the area. He was drunk! He was blitzed! And, we didn't realize this fact until we had boarded the bus and we were underway through the streets of the northern suburbs of Chicago. One of the early clues regarding his condition was when he side-swiped a couple of cars in Evanston. Shortly thereafter he managed to do a donut in an intersection hitting a couple more cars, in a forty foot bus yet! By that time we were nearing Great Lakes and it became obvious that he was racing a freight train to the crossing that led into the Main Gate. We were all in the rear of the bus singing hymns, probably *Nearer My God To Thee*. Our bus won the race to the crossing, but barely, and as we entered the Main Gate, we were met by a group of Marines who escorted our driver to the Brig. We didn't mind the walk back to our respective barracks at all.

Our basketball team traveled around the area and we played some pretty good college and service teams. One night we played Fort Sheridan in the preliminary game for a pro basketball game in Chicago Stadium. Fort Sheridan's center was a kid named Vince Boryla who was later an All-American for Notre Dame and still later was general manager for the Utah Stars. We lost, but respectably. Our basketball team was pretty good. We had high school all-staters from Illinois, Indiana and Wisconsin on our team, some sitting on the bench. That's where I spent my time during the first two games. But with a little hard work, I managed to win a starting position, at guard of all places. But any port in a storm as the saying goes. The Ninth Naval District Tournament was played on our floor and we won! And therein lies a story.

The championship game was against the Iowa City Seahawks, a preflight school at the University of Iowa composed mostly of officers and officer candidates. Their star was a kid named McCurdy from St. Johns University in New York. He was good! By halftime, they led us by 10 or 12 points and McCurdy had most of those. In the third period, there was a loose ball that was rolling toward the Seahawks baseline. McCurdy and I were in a race for the ball and I was determined to win the race. I dove for the ball just as McCurdy stooped to scoop it up. I hit him in the legs and he went rear-end-over-teakettle and hit his head on the floor. Hard. He went to the bench bleeding and didn't return. Even though I had separated my left shoulder, Coach left me in. During the fourth quarter, I exchanged a few pleasantries with Petty, their reserve center. We finally won by a point or two and as soon as the final whistle blew, I hurried to the Seahawk bench to apologize to McCurdy for the hit. Dumb decision. After apologizing to McCurdy,

I turned around only to see Petty's angry face and then the lights went out. I awoke looking at the ceiling lights and a lot of blue sleeves with gold braid. None of my teammates had seen the incident or there surely would have been a riot.

Coach rotated captains for each game, and this was my night. So still dazed from the blow, I wobbled out to accept the championship trophy from Vice-Admiral Murray, Ninth Naval District Commander. They said that I wouldn't let go of the admiral's hand at the conclusion of the ceremony.

Having won the Ninth Naval District Championship, we flew to Pensacola to play the Eighth Naval District Champions for the right to go to the All-Navy Tournament to be played at Great Lakes. Playing best of three games, we won the first game handily, barely lost the second and got clobbered in the third. I guess that we white hats couldn't cope with the good life of private rooms in the BOQ and eating all we could eat in the officer's mess in sunny Florida in the early spring.

One of the lasting memories of that tournament is of our coach, a Lieutenant SG, a southern gentlemen from South Carolina, addressing us in the Officers Club, everyone in dress blues, he giving us the do-or-die for Navy speech....with his fly open.

Taking a week off to play in the tournament meant that I had to drop back a class in school. This was my undoing. Our next assignment, secondary school, depended upon our final class standing in this school. I wanted to attend Aviation Technician's School in Corpus Christi. There were 222 guys (yes, guys, no females then) in our class. When they got to my name, there were only four of us left in the room. Corpus Christi assignments were long gone and my spirit was thoroughly crushed. So, I went to Treasure Island in San Francisco Bay. I liked it there, and I finally learned to study and did well. This was a hard lesson, but one that served me well in later life.

The base at Treasure Island occupied the old buildings that remained from the Worlds Fair that had been held there before WWII. That spring, one of these huge buildings caught fire and burned to the ground. Once again, I had the opportunity to fight fire.

Upon graduation from the school at Treasure Island, I received orders to report to the U.S.S. President Adams, APA-19 in Norfolk, Virginia, with a two week leave at home on the way. To save money, Lowell Mason and I decided to hitchhike home. Midway through this trip we found ourselves stranded on a lonely stretch of highway near Kemmerer, Wyoming. It was late at night. It was dark. It was cold. Mase had not brought his pea coat, so we took turns wearing mine. We could hear coyotes howling; at least we hoped that they were coyotes. After a few hours with no cars at all, we finally saw a train in the distance that seemed to stop about a mile from where we were standing. We hiked into town as fast as we could and luckily caught a passenger train ride into Cheyenne. From there on, it was a piece of cake. We had left Treasure Island at noon Tuesday and arrived in Park Rapids, Friday evening at 6:00 P.M., just in time to catch a ride back to Wadena to watch the PR Panthers whomp the Indians.

During the 80 hours that this trip took, we neither had the opportunity to sleep in a bed, to shave, or to change clothes. We were so tired that we were falling asleep while trying to talk to the kind people who gave us our last rides in Minnesota.

With leave over, I rode a very comfortable train to Virginia and arrived in beautiful Norfolk welcomed by signs of "Sailors and Dogs Keep Off the Grass!". I found my berth aboard the *President Adams* and we got underway that same afternoon. It was nearly two whole hours before I was seasick. This first voyage took us near the path of a hurricane off Cape Hatteras which didn't help my seasickness at all. After a few days spent at the rail on the fantail, we arrived in San Juan, Puerto Rico, and I wasn't seasick too much after that.

Our voyages were confined to the Caribbean transporting troops, families and materials with ports of call at San Juan, Puerto Rico; Colon, Panama; Port of Spain, Trinidad and Guantanamo Bay, Cuba, roughly once a month. Not bad duty.

Our first visit to Trinidad was memorable. Murphy, Radarman First Class and I are seated on the Signal Bridge. The sun has already set behind the hills just beyond the harbor where the Adams is docked but there is more than enough light to illuminate the Naval Base adjacent to the ship.

It's January, 1948. We have been in port a only few days, but quite enough time for our crew and our full load of US Marine passengers to get all personnel of the *President Adams* restricted to base for the duration of the rest of our time in Port of Spain. We are on our monthly 'milk run' into the Caribbean from Naval Bases on the East Coast of the good ol' US of A.

As you have probably guessed, the *USS President Adams* is a troop transport; but not just any troop transport. She is famous. She is one of the *Unholy Four*; four former luxury liners of the President Lines that were sequestered by the United States to serve in the South Pacific island hopping campaigns of World War II. She and her sister ships, *President Jackson, President Madison* and *Crescent City* were fast enough that they could outrun Japanese submarines. Consequently they could do their jobs of delivering troops to their invasion points without requiring destroyer escorts. Even with her coat of Navy gray and her five-inch gun mounts fore and aft, she is still quite a ship. If one looks hard enough, you can still see that she is a thoroughbred in utilitarian garb. But this all happened before I came aboard.

We have just spent most of December in the Brooklyn Navy Yard where we underwent repairs and upgrades to our equipment. We even had a replacement for the receiver and transmitter of our "Sugar-George" surface search radar; the one that I had so thoroughly screwed up during the few months that I have been attached to ship's company of the President Adams. But, that's another story.

Brooklyn Navy Yard was full of ships from the Atlantic Fleet who were there for , repairs and refits as were we. I suppose that the gray, depressing weather during December was typical of New York City at that time of year. I didn't know; it was my first time in New York. Even the Christmas lights that we could see in the distance failed to brighten our spirits. And, when Ski one of our bo'sun mates was attacked, severely beaten and robbed by a gang of locals on his way back from liberty; it did nothing to make us any happier to be in the Yard. The topper was a rare blizzard that struck a few days after Christmas dumping twenty-four inches of heavy wet snow on the city and its surrounds. Our ship's company was on port-and-starboard leave so we were at half strength: those of us who remained on board. And when the weather reports started to come in, predicting a severe storm, many of those eligible for liberty, left the ship and headed into town. That was the last that we saw of them for about a week. In the meantime the city was buried in snow. Subway traffic was stopped for days. Abandoned buses were no more than large white lumps in the streets. With twenty-four inches of 'wet and heavy' covering the ship we unlucky few were faced with clearing the decks. Think about it; we had to handle much of the snow up to four times: from the signal bridge to the flying bridge, from the flying bridge to the main deck and from the main deck, over the side. So, when our time in the Yard was finished, we were overjoyed to be underway again, and away from the cold and snow of NYC.

We made a short run down the coast to Norfolk where we picked up four hundred or so US Marine passengers bound for Guantanamo Bay and Panama and a few families as well. We were underway again after only one night in Norfolk.

Finally at sea again, on our way into the Caribbean, we had a payday! No one on board had been paid since well before Christmas. So these events were a precursor to our arrival in Trinidad a few days later. With our pockets bursting with cash, our throats parched dry and our libidos in overdrive, half of the crew and passengers of the *USS President Adams* hit the beach in Trinidad. It didn't take long for this unhappy mix of swab jockeys and jarheads to arrive at the Plaza Hotel in Port of Spain. It took even less time for hostilities to commence at the end of which, the Plaza Hotel had suffered serious damage, as had the bodies of many of the Marines and sailors. Not to mention the reputation of all of the members of the *President Adams*, all of whom were declared p*ersona non grata* for the remainder of our stay in Trinidad.

I have now set the stage for the event that I wish to relate. The evening is hot and humid, no wind. Murphy and I are enjoying the scene from our corner of the Signal Bridge, probably the coolest part of the ship at the moment. Our crew and passengers are restricted to base. But there is still the base 'slop chute' or Base Exchange where a thirsty sailor or even a Marine can quench his thirst with local beer. It is there where most of our enlisted men have retired for their evening of conversation and pursuit of cultural activities.

It is still twilight when a slight commotion is detected coming from just outside the BX. As the commotion increases a small milling group of what appeared to be US Marines are making their way slowly toward the gangway of the *Adams*. Using the high powered deck glasses on the bridge, closer examination of this phenomena reveals that, nearly lost within the melee of Marine greens, a lone figure in Navy whites sometimes appears and then disappears. Closer examination reveals that this lone figure is none other than one Michael P. Touhig, a long and lank Signalman 2nd class from the suburbs of Boston who is more than engrossed in serious conversation with about a dozen of the US Marine Corps' finest. As the group comes closer to the ship, it is that Mike is not holding up his end of the discussion. In fact, there are more and more frequent occasions when Mike is not able to hold up his end at all. Even so, it is apparent that Michael P. Touhig is slowly getting closer to the safety of the *President Adams* where surely an overwhelmingly superior force of his comrades will descend from the 'tween decks of the ship and will rescue him from his tormentors. But alas, this is not to be. We, his loyal shipmates, at least those of us who are witnessing this event, are content to remain safely onboard as onlookers only and not as active participants.

But hold; all is not lost! As luck will have it, the Officer of the Deck that evening is the colonel in charge of this detachment of Marines. As the good colonel, stationed at the head of the gangway, observes the melee arriving at the boundary of his jurisdiction, he quickly marches down the gangway onto the pier and calls this squad of Marines to "Attention!!" It takes only one such command to cause the offending Marines to form a line of ramrod straight, perfectly attired young warriors. Standing at attention, these Marines are subjected to a dressing down by their colonel such as I have not had the good fortune to hear since leaving boot camp.

Now, Michael Patrick Touhig, Signalman 2nd Class, US Navy, picks himself up from the dust and dirt of the pier, brushes himself off briefly, and feeling not bound by the authority of the Marine officer (of which he is, of course) proceeds to wreak revenge and havoc upon his now immobile assailants. Mike starts at one end of the stationary line and punches and pummels his way to the other end with nary a bit of resistance from any of the disciplined young Marines. Having completed his retribution to his satisfaction and arriving at the foot of the gangway, Mike abandons his brief crusade, sprints up the gangway and disappears into the bowels of the ship. He pauses only long enough to salute the colors and the Junior OOD and mumbles as he flies by, "Permission to Come Aboard, Sir?" Mike doesn't wait for a reply.

While in Guantanamo Bay, I was selected for Shore Patrol duty a couple of times. These were not bad assignments, generally. We were resplendent in our whites with an SP arm band, wearing a gun belt with a Colt .45 (empty of course) and a night stick. We normally went out in pairs. However, this night my job was to provide security and to keep the peace on a bus that ran from Gitmo (Navy talk for Guantanamo) to some of the small towns around the base. The bus carried Cuban nationals who worked on the base to and from their homes. The bus ran until midnight. Earlier there had been assaults and other examples of unrest on this route. There I was, a boy from a very small town in Minnesota, who didn't speak any Spanish, standing out in the crowded bus in my white sailor suit with only an unloaded .45 pistol and a puny night stick.

But, I smiled a lot and everything turned out OK.

I was discharged from the Navy in Brooklyn Navy Yard on April 6, 1948. Thus I served my country and in the process earned two years of college via the GI Bill. I did not succumb to pleadings to join the Navy Reserve and consequently avoided being called back during the Korean conflict. I felt bad about that but recovered rather quickly from my disappointment.

Many years later, my stepson, Cary Anderson, then serving in the US Navy on board the Guided Missile Cruiser *USS Antietam* CG-54, invited me to join him on what is called a Tiger Cruise. The *Antietam* was returning from six months in the Persian Gulf and in the Arabian Sea where they loitered for many weeks waiting for the go ahead, which never came, to lob a few Tomahawk missiles at Osama Ben Laden who supposedly was camped somewhere in Afghanistan. But that is another story entirely.

Eagerly accepting the invitation, I met Cary and his ship in Pearl Harbor and rode with him back to their home base in San Diego. It was a great ride, far different than my days on the *President Adams*. My quarters were an air-conditioned bunk in the chief's spaces. We were served great food. We were given tours of most of the spaces on the ship and learned about the incredible technology that propelled, navigated and armed this ship. We were given demonstrations of many of the weapons and information systems on board, some of which I had helped to develop years before at UNIVAC Defense Systems.

It took a week of leisurely cruising to transit the Pacific waters between Hawaii and Southern California. Claudia was waiting on the pier with hundreds of other family members and friends of the crew to greet *Antietam* as she led the battle group into port. We were preceded into the channel and under the bridge by a fireboat putting up towering arcs of water in celebration of the battle group's return. A huge garland resembling flowers was draped across the bows of the CG-54. Thousands of sailors in their dress whites manned the rails of the *Antietam* and of the *Kitty Hawk* and the other ships in the battle group completed this impressive display of Naval power and might. We disembarked to cheers of the families waiving signs and banners with messages and greetings and to music from a Navy band. This was truly a moving and unforgettable experience.

Boot Camp Great Lakes 1946

Receiving Trophy 1947

Great Lakes BB Team

USS President Adams

Chapter X

College and Beyond…

"A friend is one to whom one can pour out the content of one's heart, chaff and grain together, knowing that the gentlest of hands will take it and sift it, keep what is worth keeping, and, with the breathe of kindness, blow the rest away."

George Eliot

These are some 'during and after high school' stories and facts. Like the others, these are all true and if it sometimes sounds like I'm bragging, being self serving or name dropping, perhaps I am. But if I didn't relate these stories and small histories here, they probably would be lost forever. I'm proud of them (most of them) and I hope that you get as much pleasure from reading them as I do in telling them.

I must tell you a couple of summer stories. One

summer, Bob McFarren and I worked as surveyors helpers for the Hubbard County Surveyor. Most of the summer was spent in planning and improving a road in eastern Hubbard County near Lake Shingobee. It was fun work, not demanding, and we worked outside all day unless the weather was bad. We always took an hour for lunch and while the boss napped, Bob and I would look for wild strawberries. I doubt that many of my readers have had the privilege of sampling these small, rich tasting berries. Don't pass up the opportunity if you get a chance.

But I'm leading up to a dastardly trick that Bob perpetrated on me, his friend and coworker. We were running cross sections on the old road. This was a two man (sorry) two person operation with one person operating the level and the other handling the rod and the other end of the tape. This day, Bob was running the level and I the rod, which entailed heading off into the brush on either side of the road, hopefully at right angles to the centerline of the road. When I got out of line, Bob would direct me with hand signals to bring me to the proper location. At one point this afternoon, I felt that Bob was directing me further and further off line. As I was passing the tape around a clump of tall brush I realized, too late, that this was indeed the case. There, directly in front of my face, about a foot away was a large hornets' nest. The hornets discovered me at the same time as I saw them and proceeded to make me pay for the intrusion. They stung me on the head and neck a number of times even finding their way under the hat that I was wearing. I would cheerfully have killed, Sweet Old Bob, my 'friend' at that moment had my head not hurt so badly that I couldn't see him.

Another unpleasant event occurred the summer following my exit from the Navy. We had run out of surveying type activities so Don Henry and I were given a 'make work' assignment to clean out a drainage ditch on the northwest side of Fish Hook Lake. The ditch was about ten feet wide and varied in depth from knee deep to chest deep or more. Our job was to cut out brush and other obstacles that had grown into the ditch and was obstructing water flow. Working in water that deep without waders or proper equipment was bad enough, but the ditch was full of leeches. Not just the little ones, but big bloodsuckers up to five inches long. These disgusting creatures would only be discovered when one removed ones shirt, or socks, and yes, worst of all, ones trousers. After a few hours of this, Don and I agreed that this kind of work was above and beyond the call of duty and far beyond the meager wages that we earned. We should have been grateful for the work and for the job, but alas, this day we were not. So cleaning off the leeches one last time, we shouldered our tools and dripping wet hitch hiked back into town. We didn't get fired, but our boss wasn't too happy. Summer was nearly over anyway.

Just a couple more unrelated stories: Park Rapids had a very small police force and only one police car. When one needed police assistance, the procedure was to call the telephone operator who would then turn on a light above the telephone office, thereby summoning the officer on duty. Mobile radios were non-existent then. At night the officer on duty, could generally be found in his car, parked in the center lane at the south end of Main Street. The reason that he selected this spot was so that he could watch the before mentioned 'call light'. Since there normally was not very much activity at night, it was not uncommon for the officer 'on duty' to fall asleep while parked in his police car. This was true on the evening of the story that I will now relate. Bennie Noland, Park Rapids only All-State football player at that time (this has nothing to do with the story but I thought that I'd just throw that in) or maybe it was Harley Rex (my memory fails me on this one), had just returned from a hitch at Camp Rucker in Alabama. He had returned with a few simulated artillery charges from the obstacle course at Rucker. As we drove around PR looking for something to do, it was decided to wake up the pride of the Park Rapids Police Force. As we drove slowly past the sleeping officer, one of these charges was rolled under the police car and we continued slowly on. If there were a record category in the Guiness Book for speed of exit from a parked police car, that record would certainly have been broken that night.

Flushed with excitement for one successful venture, our carload of adventurers proceeded to Dodge Inn, the local 'night club'. It was Saturday night and Dodge Inn was rocking. The plan was that one of us would throw one of the artillery charges onto the roof of the one story building, and the rest of us would go inside to observe the anticipated panic. After a few minutes, the thrower came inside to get a report from us. Unbelievably, we had not heard the explosion over the hubbub of the crowd, and if anyone else had heard it they did no more than turn their heads and continued on with their revelry. Thus continued a typical Saturday night at Dodge Inn.

Buzzer Wilkins and Craig Campbell were our resident scientists and unofficial technical wizards. One Saturday evening on Main Street small groups of people were gathering together and looking into the dark sky overhead where a dim flickering light could be seen hovering over Main Street. If one listened carefully, a tinkling sound could be heard together with a rustling noise. Failing to solve the mystery or to identify the phenomena, the groups eventually dispersed, shaking their heads over the strange light and the sounds that would not go away. The truth was eventually revealed. Buzzer and Craig had built a very large box kite, equipped it with a lantern and a cowbell and had launched it upwind from Main Street using about 2,000 feet of kite line. The day before, while testing the concept in a wind that was a little too strong, the kite nearly took off with Fats, Buzzer's little brother, dragging him for a few hundred feet across a pasture as Buzzer and Craig ran to retrieve him and the kite, the kite first I think.

You may understand some of these bizarre activities a little better when you consider that we didn't have TV in those days. So what were red-blooded youths to do with their spare time?

I was discharged from the Navy on April 6, 1948; returned home and ran a resort paper route, delivering *The Minneapolis Star Tribune* to resorts and summer homes around Park Rapids. That fall I started college at Bemidji State Teachers College in Bemidji where I was planning to become a coach. I played basketball and ran track there. I was a mediocre athlete, but I did hold the Minnesota State College high jump record for a number of years. I almost went out for football. On the day that I went down to the equipment room to draw my equipment, I met George Dragich, a large lineman from the Iron Range, coming out of the locker room. He was heavily taped and bandaged. At that moment I decided that it would be prudent to concentrate on my studies and on some of the more gentile sports.

My logic may have been faulty, however. As it turned out, I suffered more severe injuries in basketball and track than I ever had in football. My basketball injuries were mostly of the ankle sprain variety coupled with a tooth displacement and few nose and other facial injuries and the separated shoulder at Great Lakes. And, I was knocked unconscious once by none other than Phil Feir who played tackle on the Army team that included the legendary Doc

Blanchard and Glen Davis. What an honor to be cold-cocked by such an athlete! But my worst injuries came in track while pole vaulting. We wore half-inch spikes on our track shoes, and on two different occasions, I ran a spike on my left shoe into that calf of my right leg as I struggled over the bar. And I severely damaged my left knee trying to learn to vault with the 'new' aluminum poles.

The following year, at the advice of government counselors, I transferred into a pre-engineering course of study, and in 1950, I transferred to North Dakota Agricultural College, now North Dakota State University, in Fargo. My first stop was at the office of Chuck Bentson, NDAC's basketball coach fresh from playing guard for Ernie Shelton on Wyoming's NCAA Championship Team. Chuck said that I could try out for his team and he would even furnish lodging for me. I declined the 'generous' offer of lodging when I visited the quarters in the basement of the men's dorm. It was a huge, dark room occupied by hulking members of the football team. In order to have a quiet place to study, I found a room in the basement of a residence across the street where I shelled out $10.00 per month for the privilege.

At NDAC, I thoughtfully made the career establishing decision to pursue electrical engineering. This crucial decision should have been made because of a burning desire to become a EE, but alas, it was made because I could, supposedly, graduate sooner than in any other major. Once again, God in His Wisdom, nudged me in the right direction.

Also, at NDAC, I courted and married Beverly Jean Widdifield on September 9, 1951 at the Presbyterian Church in Fargo. We began our married life living in one of the small expanded trailers located on what is now the Mall between the Old Men's Dormitory and the Home

Management House. With Beverly, I was privileged to help raise five great children: Janet Marie Effertz now of Bismarck, North Dakota; Robert Donald Edam of Edina, Minnesota; Catherine Ann Edam of Aurora, Colorado; Karen Jean Packard of Boulder, Colorado; and John David Edam of St. George, Utah. I consider these fine men and women to be my greatest contribution to the future of mankind and my sole claim to fame.

I graduated with a BS in Electrical Engineering in April 1953. With my new diploma, I began practicing my profession working for General Electric in Brockport and Syracuse, New York and Fort Wayne, Indiana. I returned to Minnesota in 1954 and worked for Engineering Research Associates and then General Mills and Minnesota Pipe Line Company. I rejoined ERA which eventually became Sperry UNIVAC and I worked for them in St. Paul and then in Salt Lake City. I worked for Universal Mobility Inc, and then ADDS in Salt Lake City and then in 1981 ended 29 years of working for someone else. During this time, in spite of some successes, I was laid-off, fired or demoted four times. Each time was traumatic but each was also a learning experience and provided new opportunities. In 1981, my partner, David L. Hervey, and I formed Sunbird Industries, Inc., a manufacturers representative firm that has served us well ever since. In retrospect, I changed companies too often, and I have found that working for ones self is much more satisfying than working for someone else. I probably should have done that a lot sooner.

I was privileged to meet some very interesting people during my engineering career. At Engineering Research Associates cum UNIVAC I met Seymour Cray who pioneered in supercomputers and computer aided design. At General Mills Engineering Research Division I worked for and with Dr. Karl Kober, Dr. Otmar Stuetzer, Dr. Hans

Raabe and Fritz Priekschadt all German scientists who had worked for Hitler making rockets at Peenemunde. Later, while in Salt Lake City, I was privileged to know Burt and Dick Rutan and Jeanna Yeager who planned, designed, and built the Voyageur aircraft that Dick and Jeanna flew around the world non-stop without refueling. I was invited to attend the rollout of the Voyageur aircraft at Mojave when it was introduced to the world. While at UNIVAC, I met some pioneers in the development of semiconductors: Dr. Robert Noyce, Charlie Sporck, Wilf Corrigan and others. Also at UNIVAC, I was privileged to work on both Gemini and Apollo space programs where I witnessed a few launches and met some of the astronauts. Those were interesting times.

On August 29, 1988, Claudia Ruth Pearson Anderson and I were married in Aspen, Colorado and I was given the opportunity and privilege of contributing to the welfare of six fine stepchildren: Jill Michelle Wells and Christopher Richard Anderson both of Sandy, Utah; Travis Jay Anderson of Salt Lake City, Utah; Blake Browning Anderson of Aurora, Colorado; Cary Steven Anderson of Castle Rock, Colorado and Debra Susanne Cook now living in Dayton, Ohio. They have enriched my life and I hope that their lives have also benefited from our relationship.

Bemidji STC BB Team 1949-50

Bemidji – 1950

Bemidji Teacher's College Track Conference high jump record 1949

Chapter XI

I Have Slipped the Surly Bonds

"Oh, I have slipped the surly bonds of earth, and, danced the skies on laughter silvered wings; Sunward I've climbed, and joined the tumbling mirth of sun-split clouds – and done a hundred things you have not dreamed of – wheeled and soared and swung high in the sun-lit silence. Hov'ring there, I've chased the shouting wind along and flung my eager craft through footless halls of air .Up, up the long delirious, burning blue I've topped the windswept heights with easy grace where never lark, or even eagle flew. And, while with silent lifting mind I've trod the high untrespassed sanctity of space, put out my hand and touched the face of God."

High Flight by John Gillespie Magee, Jr.

I've wanted to fly for as long as I can remember. And, for as long as I can remember, my chances of flying were as remote as, well, as flying. The only way that I could expect to fly was to join the United States Army Air Corps and that was my plan as I approached adulthood. With the war on, it seemed that my chances might be good. After all, Cousin Ken was a WWII Naval aviator, albeit lighter-than-aircraft. Rod Marshall was a flight instructor and owned a Piper J4 Cub. So it seemed that I might just sneak into flying via the military. But when WWII ended, neither the Army nor the Navy was taking flying enlistments. But I am leaping too far ahead in the telling of this chapter. Back to my childhood.

In a previous chapter I told how many ex-WWI pilots returned from the war and continued flying by becoming barnstormers, flying their vintage biplanes around the country, giving rides and performing daredevil stunts at county fairs and local air shows. Some of their stunts were truly 'death defying' and many did not survive some of these attempts. They did such things as wing-walking; leaping from one airplane to another while in flight; transferring from a speeding automobile to an airplane; crashing airplanes into barns and haystacks; etc. If someone could imagine the stunt, there seemed always to be a pilot crazy enough to give it a try. Some of these barnstormers even made it into the north country towns of Minnesota, even to Park Rapids. When one or sometimes two of these flyers arrived over town, they would announce their arrival by low passes over Main Street and over the residential parts of town. This was the only incentive that we kids needed. As soon as we heard the engine sounds low over our houses, we would run as fast as we could to the field on the northwest corner of PR that served as an airport. We would stand in awe as these knights of the air would land on the grass, coast to a near-stop and taxie their rickety steeds to a resting place on the periphery of the field and the wooden propellers would swing to an erratic stop. These men would step out of their cockpits wearing leather helmets and goggles and we would hang on every movement, every word, every gesture. There was not one amongst us who would not have pledged their lives and belongings to exchange places with these heroic figures. It was with one of these gallant men that I made my first foray into God's sky.

The summer was probably that of 1937. I had been pestering Mom to let me take a ride with one of these barnstormers. The price was not terribly high. Some pilots charged only a penny a pound of passenger weight. Others charged a fixed fee. Everything was negotiable. At the Hubbard County Fair that year, a Ford Trimotor flew into town, and was giving rides. Mom finally acquiesced and said that I could take a ride. Maybe she reasoned that there was safety in numbers. In any event, I headed for the airfield with my money clutched in my hand only to be informed that the Ford had been damaged in a hard landing and was not giving any more rides. I was more crushed than was the Ford Trimotor. But I was not yet defeated.

Shortly after that event, a barnstormer flew into town with a black and yellow biplane. I wish that I knew what kind it was. It might have been a Waco, but whatever it was, it was beautiful! It had two open cockpits, tandem. Once again, Mom agreed that I could go flying. I ran to the airfield as soon as I could that morning. The day was fresh and clear. There was no wind, no clouds.

I arrived at the airplane and approached the pilot. He agreed to give me a ride for fifty cents. Fifty cents! I eagerly handed over my hard-earned money and the pilot helped me into the front cockpit, strapped me in and then he settled himself into the rear cockpit. He shouted "Contact", cranked the engine which started on the first try and reached a high pitched roar as we began our takeoff role. The landing gear creaked and complained as we slowly gathered speed over the uneven sod until suddenly the ride became very smooth; and as I looked over the side of the cockpit, the earth slowly but steadily dropped away. We were flying! I was flying! I was ecstatic!

We flew north over Fish Hook River and over Fish Hook Lake. The air was smooth, and far below were the glassy waters of the lake; so clear that the sandbars at the Point were clearly visible. Fishermen looked like toys in their toy rowboats. Too soon, we turned back, flying over Main Street, over my school. Turning on final and cutting the engine to a quiet rumble, we touched down and once again the landing gear complained as we lurched and swayed over the bumpy pasture. The engine came to a stuttering stop and the pilot helped me from the cockpit. I may not have thanked him, I was so exhilarated, so eager to run home and tell Mom about this thrill of all thrills. I was hooked.

There were other aircraft that are a part of my memories of Park Rapids at that time. There was a hot air balloon that came to the Hubbard County Fair one year with a daredevil who parachuted from the gondola in front of the grandstand. There was a beautiful yellow Beech Staggerwing that one of the summer residents would fly to Park Rapids and land in the unimproved pasture that passed for our airport. He must have been a helluva pilot to land that high performance ship on that field. There were also a couple of amphibians that I think were owned by the Wyeths who had a summer home on Long Lake.

It would be many years before I reentered the vastness of the skies. But during that hiatus, my love affair with airplanes did not wane. I built models, many models. Some of them even flew. Dean Hedlund, one of our many boarders at the gray house, taught me how to build scale models from kits using balsa wood for the airframe structures, covered with tissue paper and with propellers powered by long rubber bands. The first one was a Curtis Robin, a model of a high winged monoplane that Dean used as an instructional tool. The second was also a Curtis Robin, but this time, Dean made me do it all myself. It wasn't as good as the first model but I was off and running. I built a Fokker D-VII; I built a Ryan ST and a Ryan SC; I built a Fairchild, an Aeronca, a Stinson, a Beech Stagger Wing, a Piper J4, and many, many more. I learned to build flying models that didn't resemble any commercial or military aircraft that ever existed, but these models did fly. I loved the symmetry of the uncovered structure; probably because I wasn't very good at covering and finishing the models.

I also started a scrapbook of airplane pictures cut out of newspapers and from magazines. The first pictures were of a Republic P-35 that reached over 500 miles per hour in a dive and the last pictures in the book were those flown in World War II. I collected pictures of American aircraft, British, Italian, German and Russian; pictures of anything that had wings. At that time, I thought that I knew them all. I have found subsequently, that I hadn't even scratched the surface. There were so many. But I still remember many of them and treasure the memories.

My next flight was when I was a senior in high school. I had broken the first joint of the pinkie finger on my right hand playing softball. Unattended to, it was healing badly and when basketball season started, it had become painful. Dr. Eiler had offered to treat the pain by removing the first joint. With that suggestion, I put my hand in my pocket, left his office and sought another solution. Rod Marshall had a doctor friend in Brainerd and offered to drop me off there when he was flying his Piper Cub down to the cities. So he did, and the doctor put my finger in a soft cast, I hitchhiked back to PR and the immobilized digit soon became useful again.

My first extended flight occurred in the Navy when our Great Lakes Basketball Team flew to Pensacola to play for the right to represent our two Naval Districts at the All-Navy BB Tournament. On a cold, blustery morning in February, at Glenview NAS northwest of Chicago, our team crowded into a Navy R4D, the Navy version of the venerable Douglas C47 affectionately called The Goonie Bird; many of which are still flying. The heating system on this aircraft was poor and we were all very cold as we headed south. There was a large vent that dispensed some heat and we each took turns huddling in front of the vent for a modicum of comfort. As we reached the red clay country of northern Alabama, the unstable air from rising thermals caused the old ship to pitch and twist and many of us were on the verge of airsickness. But before we succumbed to these unpleasant sensations, we landed at the Pensacola Naval Air Station. We taxied to the ramp and the aircraft door opened as the balmy breezes of the Gulf of Mexico wafted their hibiscus scented vapors into our still chilled red-nosed senses. We were instantly in love with the warm air, with the palm trees, with the flowers, with Florida. This love affair was probably our undoing, because as related previously, we lost the three game playoff series and returned to Great Lakes defeated, but forever enlightened, nevertheless.

Again, years passed before I was allowed to fly again. This time, I was a senior in college, and Du Pont, as a part of their effort to recruit my untried engineering talents, flew me to Wilmington, Delaware on a United Air Lines Martin 202, propeller driven air-liner. On the way as well as on the return trip, we stopped in Chicago, Midway Airport, and at Pittsburgh. This was the first of many trips by air made in behalf of and paid for by various companies that employed me in the succeeding years. I was impressed and I was on my way!

I loved flying in those years. I loved the beauty of the air. I loved the beautiful airplanes. I loved being catered to by capable and friendly stewardesses (now referred to as flight attendants, who can be of any gender, some of uncertain gender, and some even cordial). In these blissful skies, I traveled more than a million miles, probably more than two million, logging over 100,000 miles per year for many years. But those days and miles are, sadly, gone forever.

Today, thanks to the Al Qaida, to the FAA and to the airlines, we are forced to stand in line for hours in the terminal as our bodies and even our shoes (what will be next) are searched and x-rayed and our bodies patted and poked. (During this interminable process, don't even think about mentioning the word "b-o-m-b" or carry anything more dangerous than a ball point pen. Assuming that we are then allowed onboard, we are strapped into seats too small for any movement more vigorous than shallow breathing. We may (if we are lucky) be fed feasts of crackers and perhaps even peanuts and allowed to pay $3.00 for a small bottle of cheap wine (anything to dull the senses.) In the meantime, Al Qaida agents, if present, probably skip the search process, fly first class, and are afforded all of the privileges that we used to enjoy in the good years past. I'm exaggerating, obviously, but what I'm trying to convey is the fact that flying, which used to be fun, has now reached the level of traveling by Greyhound Bus. Every time I enter DIA or any other airport, I am infuriated by the thought of the millions of man-hours of productivity that are lost in the U.S. every day because air travelers must arrive at the airport an hour or two early, in order to be searched and otherwise humiliated if we are to be allowed to pay for the privilege of flying in a cattle car environment to our destination. Let's face it, it just ain't fun any more. Sometimes, I think that the terrorists have already won.

But wait, there is still some hope. There is still private aviation; although probably not for much longer.

In 1972, I finally learned to fly, at age 44. Moral; you're never too late to do something that you really want to do.

I made the impromptu but supremely great decision to take a demonstration ride in a sailplane; a glider, an airplane without an engine for you folks in Rio Linda. It was at a Sperry Management Conference in Phoenix when we chanced to spend some time at the Estrella Gliderport. (It's a long story.) Anyway, Dan Brophy and I paid our money and crowded into the rear seat of a Schwiezer 2-32 all metal sailplane and towed up to a nearby ridge. There our pilot released our ship from the tow plane and we, literally soared like an eagle for half an hour. It was beautiful. I was hooked again.

As it turned out, George Marks, one of the engineers at UNIVAC in Roseville was a glider instructor. He encouraged me to join the Red Wing Soaring Club based at Benson International Airport in White Bear Lake. Never heard of Benson International? I'm not surprised. BIA is (and maybe still is) a short grass strip off the northeast shore of White Bear Lake, with tall trees at one end and telephone wires and the lake at the other. The main feature of the 'flight operations center' was an old barber's chair that John Benson, chief pilot and owner used as his throne when he was not flying. John generally flew a Piper Super

Cub as a tow plane but could fly anything. George taught me to fly in a Schweizer 2-33 fabric covered high winged monoplane glider although my first hour of 'stick and rudder' instruction was in a good old yellow Piper J4 Cub piloted by a club member who flew 747s for Northwest Airlines in his spare time. He also owned a red Pitts Special, a single seat, high performance, aerobatic biplane that nearly killed him shortly thereafter. George was a very patient instructor and tolerated my seeming inability to maintain the proper position behind the tow plane. But eventually it all came together and I was able to 'fly on tow' and soon thereafter, mastered the art of landing on the designated airstrip. (You only get one chance in a glider, you know.)

You have probably heard stories of the elation that is related to a pilot's first solo. Whatever you have heard about the feeling of freedom; of mastery of the air, of becoming a creature never before heard of; that feeling can not be exaggerated. Even as I think about those few minutes of my first solo, I cannot begin to find suitable words. All that I can say is: I wanted to do it again, and again, and again.

Thus began a love affair with soaring that still exists today. When UNIVAC transferred me to their operations in Salt Lake City, they had, unintentionally I'm sure, sent me to the Garden of Eden of Soaring. I didn't start flying right away because I first had to learn my new job at UNIVAC. And quite frankly, I was somewhat afraid of approaching this new level of soaring. This was a whole new ballgame. This was mountain flying. These were well known soaring pilots at The Utah Soaring Association who flew out of Heber Valley Airport. There was Frank Kelsey, Soaring Hall of Fame, who built the first glider in Utah. There was Gary Flandreau, Dr. Flandreau ME professor at the

University of Utah, if you please, who conceived of and calculated the gravity skipping orbits of the first Voyager Missions to the outer planets. There was Dick Bean who still lives and breaths flying. There was Lee Steorts one of the deans of soaring in Utah who is still flying a tow plane at Heber. There were F-16 pilots from Hill AFB and many other fine pilots that I had read about in *Soaring Magazine.*This was the major leagues of soaring and there were volumes to learn, for me, a flat land glider pilot who had never flown as high as these guys towed.

The zenith of soaring is cross-country flying. It's demanding, because of the planning that must precede any cross-country flight. It is exciting because if you run out of lift en route and are unable to reach an airport, you must 'land out'. In other words, you must find some alternative landing site, a pasture, a golf course, a road, any place where you and your ship can safely land. There is a saying at Heber Valley: "There are two kinds of glider pilots in Utah, those who have landed out and those who will land out." Boy, were they right!

During my years in Utah, I landed out on five different occasions. The first time was in a field west of the airport; (I almost made it back to the field) then in another field near Santaquin (nowhere near an airport); next was on a road north of Duchesne (broke an axle on this one); fourth was a pasture next to Scipio (that fence was really close); and lastly on the Park City golf course (planned).

But, before being cleared for cross-country flight at Heber Valley, I first had to circumnavigate the valley at Heber traversing the ridges surrounding the valley. Having received check rides in the club's Schweizer 2-22, and having transitioned into the club's Schweizer 1-26, a medium performance single-place sailplane, I was ready. On that day, I towed up to the Wallsburg ridge south of

Heber, where most of our soaring adventures generally began. There in the Wallsburg valley, about a mile away, was the largest dust devil that I have ever seen before or since. This dust devil extended from the valley floor, far above my release altitude of over 7,000 feet. I flew over to this phenomena and immediately found strong lift at its periphery. Circling a few hundred yards from the center of this funnel shaped rising column of dust, I was lifted to an altitude of over 16,000 feet in what seemed to be only a few minutes. This seemed to be too easy. I had donned my oxygen mask as I climbed and then left this area of strong lift and proceeded to circumnavigate the valley, an easy task with this high altitude start. As I flew around Heber City and Midway my lips and my elbows began to tingle and I noticed that my finger nails were turning blue. My oxygen regulator was not working and I was experiencing altitude hypoxia for the first time. I gradually descended to a more oxygen rich altitude as I returned to the airport. I was not in danger at any time, but rather added to my knowledge of potential risks that accompany mountain flying. And, I was now certified to take the Club's ships on cross-country flights.

About this time, Gary Flandreau and I became partners in a Standard Libelle 301 fibre glass sailplane, tail letters GA that we affectionately called Green Apples. This was an early 15-meter sailplane built in Germany and previously owned by Gary Able of Boulder, Colorado. With a L/D (glide ratio) of over 30 to 1, this was a serious soaring machine. I was ready for cross-country flying.

But, I made my first out landing before I even attempted my first cross country flight. This was very embarrassing. I had been giving rides to friends and relatives in the Club's 2-33 for some time, since I was certified by the Club's Safety Officer. I was giving a ride to

Colleen Brophy, our friends' daughter. We had towed to the Wallsburg ridge and had released in lift. I flew into the Wallsburg valley to join two other ships that were obviously thermaling. As I reached the area, the other ships left and I could find no lift. I immediately headed back to the ridge. No lift there either, and to my extreme chagrin, I was below the level of the ridge and on the wrong side from the airport. I began flying down the ridge in order to fly around the end so that I could return to the airport. When I was finally able to turn the corner and had the landing strip in sight, it was obvious, even to me, that I didn't have enough altitude to make it back. I was going to make my first out landing:

Pick out a field and do it now! There is a good looking field straight ahead, but it's guarded by a row of tall poplars and I am below tree top level. There is a gap between two of the trees that looks like I can fly through and reach the field. But is it really wide enough for my wings to make it through? I'm not sure. This is crazy! At the last moment I change my mind and abort this idea. I'm going to be on the ground in just a few seconds. Where will I land? I bank to the left and select a small field guarded by a barbed wire fence and an irrigation ditch. With scarcely time to think, I dive at the fence, zoom over it, touch down briefly and bounce across the irrigation ditch and skid to a stop just short of the next fence. We made it. It wasn't pretty, and I certainly wasn't proud of it, but we made it. No damage. No one injured. And another lesson learned: always, always have a plan to deal with any emergency than can occur in the next moment.

The next out landing was a little less frantic. I was attempting my first cross-country, a planned flight from Heber Valley to Evanston, Wyoming, a distance of a little over 50 air miles. In the air, I changed my mind and headed south with the idea that I would fly to Nephi about the same distance. Bad idea. With decent altitude I flew down Spanish Fork Canyon with the thought that I could find ridge lift and proceed down the Wasatch front to the Nephi area. As I turned the corner into the valley, I encountered a rain squall and dead air beyond it. I struggled for altitude for a few minutes and then resigned myself to the inevitability of my second out landing.

I fly further west into the valley looking for a suitable field. There are a few good ones. Pick one out; I'm getting low. Which way is the wind coming from? There are no tell tales but probably from the south. Turn south. I'm skidding; ease off on the rudder. Good air speed; maybe a little fast. We're on final for that big mowed field beyond the power lines. Gear down. Spoilers out. Flare and touch down. Let my momentum carry me over to the fence by the road. I'm down and safely.

I get on the radio but I can't reach Heber because of the mountains. A local boy arrives and gives me a ride into Santaquin on the back of his motorcycle. I call Heber and arrange for Lee and Gary to bring the trailer and get a ride back to the ship. Before Lee and Gary arrive, a thunder storm strikes and I sit in the cockpit while the thunder storm rages, with the ship turned into the wind in order keep it on the ground during the wind gusts. Gary and Lee arrive and we trailer back to Heber. John and Max are waiting for me in the 280Z and, although hungry, are OK. I buy dinner for everyone and we all go home. This time, except for poor planning, I did everything right. More lessons learned.

The next out landing was more exciting. I had planned an FAI Diamond 300 km out and return attempt between Heber and Vernal. Everything was going well until I encountered a rain squall north of Duchesne. Once again, the squall squelched local lift and I was frantically searching for any air going up. Instead of working my way south to better landing possibilities around Duchesne, I chose to venture into a canyon leading up into the high Uintahs in search of ridge lift. Bad decision. Nothing was going on and I was forced to turn around and fly back down the canyon. I had spotted an unpaved road along the east side of the canyon that could offer what appeared to be a possible landing place. Most of the road was tight up against the sloped canyon wall, so that there was no room for the tips of the Libelle's long wings. In one spot, however, there was about 100 yards of road where the banks sloped away on both sides. I headed for that.

I am losing altitude as I approach the chosen section of road which looks even smaller as I get closer. The topography drops away south of this section and I don't know what is on the other side. I might be able to trade the elevation change for more distance, but the possibilities might not be any better. So the road it is. I lower my landing gear, pop the spoilers and aim for the closest part of the selected area. I'm a little high and the end of the safe section is approaching rapidly. I don't dare bounce because we will certainly overshoot. So I fly it onto the road and apply the brakes to hold it down. A loud grinding noise! We skid to a stop much faster than expected! I open the canopy and step out still wearing my parachute. Old Green Apples is wounded. She's resting on her belly with the landing gear doors squashed beneath her, the wheel at an odd angle. I find a portion of the axle along the side of the road. Either the axle was cracked or I landed her too hard. I pull her off the road and stop to consider my plight.

I'm probably 20 miles from any telephone. I can't raise Heber on the radio because of the mountains to the west. I need a telephone but I don't know which way is best to go, so I decide to hitch a ride with the first car that comes by. About half and hour later a car is approaching from the south. Two young girls are in the car. They are going to a resort at the top of the canyon which has a radio-telephone. We reach the resort but the guy with the radio telephone is not there. So nothing to do but wait. A group of men at the bar want to hear my story and insist on buying me a drink. I acquiesce. It's been a hot dry day so far. Finally, the guy with the radio telephone arrives and I'm able to reach Heber. There's no one there to come and get me. So I finally reach Paul and Karen and tell them where to find me. Since I'm only 10 or 11 miles up hill from the ship, I decide to hike down the mountain to meet them. I finally reach the ship. I'm dehydrated and hot, feeling a little disoriented. Paul and Karen arrive just as the sun is going down. We disassemble Green Apples and wrestle her into the trailer, which is made difficult because of her fractured undercarriage. We drop her off at Heber and proceed home. Not a flight to be proud of.

The next out landing occurred on a club cross country attempt from Nephi to Cedar City, Utah. We arrived early at the Nephi, airstrip, four ships, assembled our trusty steeds and waited for the lift to develop. About 11:00 AM small puffs of cumulus clouds began to appear over the low ridge west of the airport. As club president at that time, it was my job to explore the lift and report back when it was strong enough to proceed. So I donned my parachute, strapped myself into Green Apples and towed up to the ridge. I released in weak lift and proceeded to fly up and down the ridge looking for stronger thermals. After 30 minutes or so, the lift became encouraging enough to proceed, so I advised my fellow flyers on the ground and Green Apples and I headed south. Lift was spotty and not strong but appeared to be getting stronger as the day progressed. Just west of Sevier Reservoir, I began to lose altitude over some new freeway construction. I was down to about 2,000 feet AGL and began looking for a suitable place to land. Nothing looked very good and as I was preparing to land on the newly graded freeway surface, I discovered a strong thermal and climbed a few thousand feet and resumed my journey south. As I approached Scipio, the lift diminished once again. I knew that there was good terrain south of the divide at Scipio, if I could just clear the ridge. In an effort to gain the necessary altitude, I flew west toward a large mountain there looking for ridge lift or for another strong thermal. Alas, I guessed wrong again, and flew back toward Scipio looking for a suitable field. There were a few small pastures west of town so I picked one, flew base leg over town, turned final, and descended steeply over a stand of poplars onto the pasture. We touched down in soft earth and came to a halt about 20 yards from the other end of the pasture. By radio, I reported the condition of the field to my compatriots who had run out of gas also. Mark Emeley in his BG-12 was next to land and landed safely. Russ Worrell in his home built sailplane was next glider to follow Mark. For some unknown reason, Russ landed very short and flew into the barbed wire fence at the edge of the field. One strand of barbed wire came into the cockpit destroying the canopy and cutting a deep gash in Russ's shoulder. The last of our group Chuck Rockwell in his Dart was lost; it took his crew hours to find him miles west of Scipio. They didn't arrive in Cedar City until well after dark, when the rest of us had finished dinner and at least one libation.

My last off field landing was really planned, since the Club agreed to participate in an air show in Park City. Three of us towed from Heber to the ridges above Park City and then loitered until their improvised ground control guy invited us to land on a fairway of the golf course. I was second to land and although I was a little long and a little fast, I had no difficulty in stopping short of a sand trap. My friend John Mildon was not so lucky. John, flying the Club's Schwiezer 1-34, was way high on final and instead of forcing the ship down, attempted to go around. Breaking a cardinal rule of soaring, John hooked a wing tip as he made a steep bank at a much too low altitude. He cart wheeled the ship and was very fortunate to escape with moderate back injuries. The 1-34 was not so lucky and was out of commission for a number of months.

Another disconcerting event that occurred as I landed was that a group of sky divers touched down within yards of where I landed just as I stopped rolling. I didn't see them and didn't know that they were in the air. A recipe for disaster.

You may be getting the idea that soaring is a hazardous hobby. It can be. There had been one recent death at Heber Valley before I joined the Club. A German tow pilot was giving the first aircraft tow to a sailplane pilot experienced in winch tows only. Takeoff techniques are quite different. The sailplane pilot pitched up steeply the moment that he was airborne, lifting the tow planes tail and causing it to nose into the runway. The tow pilot would probably have survived had he fastened his seat belt.

There were three fatalities while I flew at Heber. A student was flying solo with the club's 1-22 on the Wallsburg ridge and panicked as he lost altitude. Trying to reach the airport by crossing the ridge with insufficient altitude, he clipped a tree, went inverted and was killed.

A lady from Las Cruces was buying a sailplane for her husband's birthday. He had agreed to buy the BG-12 from Dick Bean and Mark Emeley. The deal was struck and the young man was test flying the sailplane. Everything appeared to be normal until the ship was on final and almost at the runway threshold when it pitched down and was nearly inverted when it crashed. Neither the ship nor the pilot survived. The ship had passed inspection only days before. An autopsy showed that the young man had terminal cancer. A suicide? Quite likely. And, poor Dick and Mark lost their ship as well as the agreed upon sale price.

In the last fatal incident, an experienced sailplane pilot from California had driven all night to test fly Bob Preece's RS-15 that was for sale. He was flying at about 4,000 feet AGL over Deer Creek Reservoir when he suddenly entered a vertical dive and crashed into the reservoir. Why? No one knows.

There were a number of other close calls, but I won't bore you with them here, except for one that involved me. One weekend I had towed Green Apples behind my 280Z up to Haley, Idaho near Sun Valley to fly with some folks from Seattle. I made two very bad landings there, but nearly 'bought the farm' on the first morning. I had taken a low tow onto the ridge just east of the airport and was flying up and down the ridge in weak ridge lift a few hundred feet above it. I was looking over the side of the cockpit studying the terrain below, looking for lift producing features. I happened to look up and there, in freeze frame, was another sailplane on a collision course with me and only a few hundred feet away. We were closing at over 120 miles per hour. I had less than a second to pop the stick forward and pass under the ASW-19 with no more than ten feet separating the two ships. There was no time to think or to be afraid, only time to react. Had I not looked up at that moment, the sky would have been filled with bits of fiber glass and the remains of two unfortunate pilots. Hours later, after we had landed and were discussing our flight, the other pilot revealed that she had not seen me until I was passing underneath. A very lucky day in our respective lives.

Those years that I was privileged to fly with the members of the Utah Soaring Association were wonderful years. The members were great guys and became good friends as well. Saturdays were the best days of the week. Club members would arrive at the Heber airport mid morning or earlier and would began to assemble our ships, helping each other as necessary. Instrumentation was checked, water bladders were filled, etc. We would discuss what we expected from the day, what the weather might be and any cross country flights that anyone might be planning. Then we would retire to some shade, eat a light lunch and wait for the day to 'begin'. When it began to be apparent that thermals were beginning to work, there would be a line of ships formed at the end of the runway waiting for a turn to tow out. On most days, we would be in the air for at least a couple of hours and perhaps as long as five or six. Then about 4:30 PM we would get a call on our glider frequency from Bob Preece in his motor home near the hangars: "It's Miller time!" Bob would declare, and the chickens would start to come home. As each ship landed and was wrestled back to their respective places on the ramp, the snap of pop-tops on Coors cans could be heard as we disassembled our ships and discussed the day's flights. Non-beer drinkers will have difficulty understanding how good that first beer tasted! We were all dehydrated from the long hours on the asphalt ramp under the Utah high altitude sun coupled with a few hours on oxygen if the day was really good. That first cold beer was ambrosia indeed.

Bob Preece passed away of a sudden heart attack while he and his second wife had the motor home across the border in Mexico. The Mexican authorities would not allow his body to be returned to the U.S. so his wife had Bob cremated and she crossed the border with his ashes in a drawer in the motor home. Bob had neglected to change his will following his second marriage so his wife returned to Utah practically destitute. In lieu of a funeral, Frank Kelsey suggested that Bob's friends in the soaring club hold an informal memorial service in Heber and then scatter his ashes over the Wallsburg ridge where Bob had spent many happy hours in this RS-15. His wife agreed and we proceeded.

We met the next Saturday morning in a small restaurant in Heber City near the airport. The day was overcast and gray, very appropriate for the task at hand. After breakfast and following a group conversation wherein we recalled Bob and many stories related to him and his years with the club, we all proceeded to the airport to witness the scattering of the ashes. The plan was for Frank and Dick Bean, then club president, to fly Bob's ashes to the ridge in Frank's Schweizer 2-32 and scatter the ashes along the crest of the ridge. Frank, ever creative, had devised a long narrow aluminum box with spring loaded covers at each end. Bob's ashes were placed in this box and the box secured to the top of the 2-32's wing near the wing root. The theory was that at the appropriate time, Dick Bean would open the box covers with a lanyard from the cockpit and the slipstream would release Bob over the terrain where he flew so many times. So much for theory.

We on the ground observed Frank, Dick and Bob (in the box) tow up to the ridge and release over it. Then we observed a series of uncharacteristic and semi-violent maneuvers of the 2-32 up on the ridge. After a short time, the maneuvers ceased and Frank and Dick, together with Bob still in the box, returned to the airport and landed.

It seems that Frank had failed to consider the vacuum

that occurs over the upper surface of an airfoil when in flight. All went well until Dick pulled the lanyard and opened the doors to Bob's box-urn. Sans slipstream, Bob declined to leave the solitude of his airborne coffin. Repeated numbers of rolls, pitches and yaws and even a few whifferdills, were unable to disturb him from his rest. So returning to the airport and relying on time tested manual methods, Bob's remains were forever ensconced along the runway that he loved so much. He actually had spent most of his time there anyway, drinking Miller Lite. I have an idea that during this entire escapade, Bob was looking down upon our futile efforts and smiling… probably with a beer in his hand.

May I relate a few flights that I'm proud of. Our soaring club had planned a weekend flying out of Driggs, Idaho, in the shadow of the Grand Teton. Lee Steorts, my partner in Green Apples, at that time, and I flipped to see who would attempt to fly from Heber to Driggs and who would attempt the flight back. I won the flight up and was able to complete the flight to Driggs in about six hours after I released over the Uintahs. The resulting distance was about 200 miles so my time wasn't very good but it completed my FAI Gold Distance Goal (300 km) and was very exciting. Ask me about it sometime. I love to tell the story.

Shortly after this flight I was able to climb to 25,000 feet ASL in a mountain wave above Mt. Timpanogas west of Heber getting my FAI Diamond Altitude Award. Then I completed my Diamond Out and Return by flying from Heber to Vernal, Utah and back. The flight was relatively uneventful, but satisfying never the less. Regrettably, I was never able to complete my third and last diamond, a 500 kilometer distance task.

I received my license in powered aircraft in 1986 in Salt Lake City but logged only a hundred hours or so, far fewer than I have in sailplanes. But my true love in flying was and still is in sailplanes. In my estimation, this is true flying.

My last flight in Green Apples was at Heber Valley on a warm, colorful autumn day. It was only a local flight but was fitting as it was, although I didn't know it at the time, my final soaring flight. There were snow white cumulus clouds scattered about the Heber Valley. As the day developed, there seemed to be lift everywhere. There were a number of club ships aloft, and the glider frequency was filled with chatter; flyers reporting their location, their altitude and the location of lift. One normally does not climb above cloud base because to do so generally involves flying into the cloud itself. But that day, it was possible to climb along the sides of these beautiful creations, thousands of feet above the base. I recall flying between clouds and actually putting my left wing deep into the cloud as the cockpit remained in clear blue sky and I circled the cloud. This sort of flying is strictly forbidden by the FARs, Federal Air Regulations, and Frank Kelsey, ever mindful of safety, was nearly frantic that day trying to keep his charges at approved altitudes and with proper separation from clouds and other ships. This was probably the most satisfying day of pure flying that I ever experienced. Although another flight, where I was the passenger, comes to mind.

Claudia and I were traveling in New Zealand and as we drove into Queenstown on the South Island we were greeted by the sight of a sky full of paragliders, large parachute like creations with rectangular canopies. We could see that some of these 'chutes were carrying two people. I declared to Claudia, "I'm going for a ride!"

We located the small park like field, far smaller than a city block in size, at the base of a small mountain served by a gondola. I spoke with a young man who had just landed with a passenger about the price of a ride, and he informed me that he was booked but that another young man, close by who had also just landed, would accommodate me. We agreed on a price that included passage on the gondola to the top of the mountain. I helped him pack up his craft and we entered the cable car. Stepping off of the gondola at the top, I expected that we had arrived at the departure point for the paraglider. But my pilot, doing a good imitation of a mountain goat, took off up a steep, narrow path further up the mountain. Huffing and puffing and wondering if I could forestall a coronary episode until after the ride that I had paid for, I finally caught up with my host in a small clearing at the edge of a nearly vertical cliff.

We unpacked the paraglider and spread it out on the ground with the thin shrouds reaching a point at the harness that was to be our cockpit. The young man donned his harness and helped me into mine which he then fastened to the front of his. We shuffled awkwardly to the edge of the cliff as he conversationally gave me instructions. Then, tugging on the shrouds, the canopy filled with air and remaining on our feet as long as possible, within moments, we were gently lifted into the air and off the cliff. Thus began more than a few minutes of quiet ecstasy.

The initial moments of this memorable flight took us low over the tops of pine trees of some sort that were growing along the mountainside. We gathered speed and found lift and flew out into the valley and over the city of Queenstown. The city is situated on the shore of Lake Wakatipu. The feeling of quietly transiting the city from an altitude of a few thousand feet is indescribable. It was as though I was alone and stationary, suspended in clear air, with this sunlit panorama passing slowly between my feet. We flew out over the lake shore and over an excursion steamer tied up at the dock and then back over the city toward our, soon to be, landing field. At some point I asked my pilot how long he had to train in order to get a license. His response was memorable: "Train? License?"

I felt no need to explore the subject further at this critical point. Too soon our altitude diminished and I could see Claudia far below taking pictures. Very much like landing a glider, we flew an abbreviated left-hand pattern, flying a base leg and then turning on a short final into the grassy area. I expected that at the last moment, we would flare and step lightly onto the turf. Wrong again. We approached our touch down point at what, I considered, to be a high rate of speed. My young pilot admonished me to "Keep your feet up!" Which I did, and we landed on our respective butts and skidded to a halt about fifty feet from a small equipment building. I considered doing it again, and since Claudia declined an invitation, I too decided to quit while my body was still functional.

I'll end the story telling here; I've probably bored you enough. Thanks for staying with me and with my stories until the end. As I have mentioned earlier, the next time that we meet, I would like to discuss this book and these stories with you, if you would like. Until then...........

"*May the road rise up to meet you, may the wind be always at your back. May the sun shine warm upon your face, the rains fall soft upon your fields And until we meet again, may God hold you in the palm of His hand.*"

Old Irish blessing.

Chapter XII

Where Did We Come From?

"There's a race of men that don't fit in, a race that can't stay still; so they break the hearts of kith and kin and they roam the world at will. They range the field and they rove the flood and they climb the mountain's crest. Theirs is the curse of gypsy blood and they don't know how to rest."

Author unknown

Most of us know a lot, or at least some, about our own parent's history. But how much do we know about their parents and about our parents' ancestors, and so on? Very little, I found, as I started to write this book. I've learned quite a bit since then so, I feel it necessary to relate the 'begats" of our family as best as I can at this time. If nothing else, this document may be helpful to my great-grandchildren who will inevitably be required to submit a paper to their teacher detailing their ancestry as far back as possible. Tracing ones genealogy has to be a labor of love for the searcher because at best, it is exceedingly demanding as well as frustrating. Old records are difficult, and sometimes impossible, to locate. And, many are inaccurate with misspelled or eligible names. But one does the best that one can.

There are many more Edams in the U.S. than I had imagined. A map of the location of Edams in the United States in the late 1700s and the early 1800s show them to be scattered all along the East Coast from Vermont to Louisiana. Although most of the Edam records that we have found describe individuals of European descent, some of the Edams were and are of African descent. There are records where the given name of the individual is 'Edam'. This indicates that the person may have been a slave who belonged to a slave owner also named Edam.

We have located early Edams in Europe, in Scotland, England and Germany, some dating back to the 1600s. We have found parish and probate records of John Edam in Midlothian County, Scotland in 1659, and of Bessie and Conin Edam in Wigtown County, Scotland about 1672. James Edam, a Scottish tailor left Liverpool on the *John Cumming* bound for the U.S. on May 11, 1837 but seems to have disappeared after setting foot in America. We found a record of Margaret Edam of Scotland born there in 1701. And there's more: there are burial records from Yorkshire of Rawling Edam, 1662, of *Richard ye son of Edward buried, 1671* and marriage records for Edwarde Edam to Ellinge Hedon in 1671 and of James Bird to Margaret Edam, 1675 all in Yorkshire. An 1891 census shows Helen Edam, age 31, an actress in London. And there are others who embarked from England for the United States and seemed to have disappeared upon arrival. There was a large Edam group from Baden, Bavaria who settled in Ohio near

Cleveland. And there are many more. Are these our ancestors? Some may be, but we have yet to identify them.

My mother once told me that she thought that our 'Edam' name may have been spelled 'Eidem' or 'Eidam' at one point in time and it seems that the latter is true. Claudia located some 'Eidams' near Trondheim in Norway and some 'Eidems' in Switzerland, but we believe that early Eidams came from Germany. So, while I have always thought that our name was Dutch in origin, it is most likely German.

My Sarff ancestors were certainly German, with Abraham Sarff arriving in America as a mercenary fighter in the Revolutionary War on the side of the British. The Canfield side of the family probably originated in the United Kingdom, but we have not yet discovered proof of this.

Some years ago, my son Bob made contact with an Edam family from Missoula, Montana, and we exchanged records but were unable to establish any linkage at that time. Now, with more research, it appears that their grandfather, William George Edam, is the same man, George William Edam, that we believe to be my grandfather. He was as colorful as he was elusive. Both were born in Virginia. Both were married more than once. Both were blind (in one eye as it turns out) and both were fiddlers. As the Montana Edams quip, "He was a fiddler and boy did he fiddle around!" That's my Grandpa Edam! As important as the families of these two half-brothers are to our history, it is doubtful that either knew of the others existence.

Shirley Edam of Great Falls, Montana, sent us a picture of George William that was taken around 1865 in Iowa. As you can see in the picture included in this book, George William Edam was a handsome, swash buckling young man with the look of a rapscallion. In the picture, he is holding, what I believe to be the same violin that my father left with Mom after his death. We have tried to locate this violin, but the odds are certainly against success. The bottom line is that Louis Thomas Edam and Bert Oliver Edam probably had the same father, George William (or William George) Edam, so that my dad and Bert are half-brothers. Thus, we Edams have cousins in Montana via Dodgeville, Wisconsin. Amazingly, my next-door neighbor here in Monument, is Jerry Weier, part of the Wisconsin/Montana Edam family, hence one of my distant cousins. It is a small world indeed!

We have tried to trace three ancestral lines: Sarff, my maternal grandmother's line; Canfield, the lineage of my maternal grandma's first husband; and Edam, my father's ancestry. What follows is what we know today, or at least what we're pretty certain of. These brief biographies and remembrances of these members of my family are the best and most accurate information that our research has yielded so far. Special attention is given to my immediate family, of course. We will try to update these records as new information becomes available.

Our thanks to Robert Fletcher for his research on the Sarff family in Europe and in the U.S. and to Jerome P. Daniels for his research on Fanny Daniels. Linking up with these research efforts has aided immeasurably in completing the biographies in the following pages. My cousin, Ruby Gadbaw Sartain, has contributed mightily with photos of the early Sarff and Canfield sides of the family. And Shirley and Morris Edam from Montana have provided invaluable information that is key to the linkage of our respective families.

I. SARFF ANCESTRY:

Johann George Sarff, circa 1716: This man is my great, great, great, great, great grandfather. He was born in

Germany, probably in Zwiebrucken about 1716 and married Johanna Magdalena in about 1736. She was also born about 1716.

Phillip Henry Sarff, circa 1738

Phillip Henry, son of Johann and Johanna Sarff was born about 1738 in Germany and married Anna Maria Kruger on April 11, 1758. They are my great, great, great, great grandparents.

Abraham Sarff I, 1762 – 1811

Abraham Sarff I, the son of Phillip and Anna Marie Kruger Sarff; was born in Zwiebrucken, Germany in 1762, married Katherine Kerbaugh, in Abbottstown, Adams County, Pennsylvania in 1790 and died in Little York, Pennsylvania in 1811. Katherine was born in 1770 in Pennsylvania and died there about 1845. They were farmers and are my great, great, great grandparents. According to the Todd County Historical Society publication *Todd County History*, Abraham Sarff came to America as a Hessian soldier and fought in the American Revolutionary War on the side of the British. These Hessian soldiers were called mercenaries but most of the funds paid by the British for their services went to the German Duke or to the Prince who furnished the required number of troops. These troops were recruited from certain cities or principalities in Germany; such as Zweibrucken, Prussia, Hess and Brunswig. Following their defeat at Yorktown, the British abandoned their Hessian troops so Abraham Sarff, left to his own devices, settled in Pennsylvania, married Katherine, and thus began the Sarff family in the United States.

John Henry Sarff, 1797 – 1869

John Henry was born December 22, 1797 in Little York, Pennsylvania. He married Salome Marv Hoke in 1821 in York County, PA and died October 13, 1869 in Snicarte, Mason County, Illinois; Salome was born February 17, 1800 also in Little York. The Sarffs were reputed to be very successful farmers in Pennsylvania. John Henry and Salome are my great, great grandparents.

Jonas Sarff, 1824 - 1903

Jonas Sarff, my maternal great grandfather, was born April 12, 1824 in Little York, Pennsylvania and headed west with his brothers in what history refers to as 'The Hoosier Migration'. On August 18, 1846, Jonas married Sarah Cole, my maternal great grandmother, in Randolph County, Indiana. Jonas died August 3, 1903 in Browerville, Minnesota and is buried in Evergreen Cemetery there. Sarah was born in Ohio in 1828 and died there, we think in 1870. One of their children was Alice Belle Sarff, my maternal grandmother. Following Sarah's death, Jonas continued on to Minnesota in a train of eleven oxen drawn wagons. In Minnesota, Jonas married Marie Duffney who was born in Minnesota on March 1, 1832 and died March 16, 1900. They had three children.

My cousin, Ruby Gadbaw Sartain, believes that Jonas had nine or ten brothers, some of whom were ministers in the United Brethren of Christ Church in York, Pennsylvania. It was this information that put us on track to locate much of the Sarff family history. We have traced at least six of John Henry's sons to Minnesota: Issac, Jonas, Jacob, John, Joshua and Manassas. Jonas and his brothers were homesteaders around Eagle Bend, Clarissa and Browerville, Minnesota. Jonas and his brothers became prominent citizens, ministers and businessmen in Todd County.

Alice Belle Sarff Canfield Black, 1864 – 1944

Alice Belle Sarff Canfield Black is my maternal grandmother. She was born in Adams County, Indiana and moved to Todd County, Minnesota, a few miles northeast of Browerville, when she was five or six years old. They came in a train of eleven, oxen drawn covered wagons with her father, Jonas Sarff and her uncles. She told of encountering Indians during their five-week trip to Minnesota and of being hidden in a trunk for fear that the Indians would carry her off. It turned out that the Indians were starving and women in the train fed them. A few days later the Sarffs found the freshly killed carcass of a deer outside their wagons. The Indians had apparently repaid their kindness. She and her family together with the families of her uncles, established small homesteads near Eagle Bend, Clarissa and Browerville in Todd County, Minnesota.

Grandma told of encountering a bear while walking to school one day, and that her father hunted and killed the bear which he brought home and added to the family larder. Grandma said that she especially liked the 'bear grease' on her pancakes.

Her family grew most of their food on the farm and made as many of their necessary supplies as they could. They made their own soap from wood ashes, lard or fat and lye. Grandma, mistaking a glass of lye for water, drank enough of the caustic solution to severely scar her throat. Their doctor told her that she should drink wine from time to time to treat her injury. Being a young Christian lady, she was loathe to touch the stuff, but she followed doctors orders never the less. That is probably where I inherited my taste for the grape.

Grandma and her family went to a small country church near their farm. Communion there involved passing a wine bottle amongst the communicants with each person taking a swig from the bottle and with some expressing their faith verbally. On one Communion Sunday, when the bottle reached a Native American member of their congregation, according to Grandma, he proclaimed, "Me love Jebus much!" and drained the bottle.

Even though she had only finished four grades at her country school, she was proud of the fact that she had read the Bible four times, cover to cover. She practiced her Christianity daily. There was a time in her life when she cleaned houses for a living. If she encountered a playing card in executing her duties, she wouldn't touch it. Instead she would use a broom and a dustpan to remove what she called "instruments of the devil". You can imagine how difficult it was for any of her grandchildren when we decided to learn to play cards. Any such activity had to be conducted in utmost secrecy.

And Grandma spread her ministry in other ways. Later in her life, while living in Long Prairie, one of her neighbors who lived behind her kept a whiskey bottle in the woodpile next to his lot line and to her home. Grandma was scandalized by this un-Christian behavior and decided to do her bit to nudge this man toward a more temperate life. So, she surreptitiously emptied the liquor from the bottle and refilled it with an amber fluid of her own making. What I'm trying to say is: "She peed in the bottle and put it back in the woodpile." History is silent on any forthcoming actions or reactions to her homegrown therapy and ministry.

Grandma married Will G. Canfield when she was 19 years old and gave birth to Harriet (also called Ella), Elsie (my mother) and Leo. Will died of 'brain fever' in 1897. Widowed at an early age, Grandma married Clarence Delmont Black but had no more children. Clarence Black died of Bright's Disease after a long illness ten years later.

Grandma Black was a thin, little lady when I knew her, barely five feet in height but as tough as boot leather. I can recall her chopping firewood when she was in her 70s. And she was as colorful as she was tough. Her favorite curse was “Shoot-a-button!” and a typical opinion of an inconsequential issue was, “That don’t amount to a fart in a frying pan!” Her phrase “Plague take it!” always indicated extreme agitation and suggested that we leave her to her thoughts and the problem at hand.

She had a mixed set of ancient butcher knives with blackened handles and blades worn narrow from frequent sharpening. She used these for cooking of course; but also for removing slivers and splinters from little hands and feet of any of her wards fortunate to be blessed with her daily care. Her application of iodine to the remaining wound from one of her butcher knife surgeries was a welcome relief by comparison.

Her final years were spent caring for my five cousins in a small house (still there) on Riverside Avenue in Park Rapids. My memory of her is of a tiny woman with gray hair parted in the middle, with a large bun in the back, wearing a worn dress and an equally worn apron and with a loving smile. She died January 31, 1944 with a failing memory, Alzheimers I imagine, leaving only one living child and ten grandchildren. She is buried along side my parents in Browerville, Minnesota. She was a remarkable woman. God bless you Grandma.

II. CANFIELD ANCESTRY:

Emerson Canfield, 1811 – circa 1865

Emerson Canfield is my maternal great-grandfather. He was born in either Massachusetts or Connecticut (records are eligible) and married Jane about 1840. They lived in, Minden, Montgomery County, New York at that time. Emerson and Jane, together with one child, Warren, moved to Wisconsin between 1840 and 1850 where they farmed near Hudson in Walworth County. Other children: Sarah, Francis, Calvert, Everton, Rowena, William (my grandfather) Mary and Annie were all born in Wisconsin. Emerson died there between 1860 and 1870.

Jane (or Mary Jane) Canfield – 1821 – circa 1890

Jane Canfield is my maternal great grandmother. She was born in New Hampshire and married Emerson Canfield sometime around 1840 and lived with him near Minden in Montgomery County, New York. Their son Warren was born in New York. Sometime between 1840 and 1850, she moved, with her family, to a farm near Hudson in Walworth County, Wisconsin where she lived for about 25 years. There, she gave birth to eight additional children: Sarah, Francis, Calvert, Everton, Rowena, William (my grandfather), Mary and Annie. After Emerson's death, in about 1875, Jane moved to Cedar Township in Floyd County, Iowa, where she lived with her son Everett, his wife Carrie and their children Harry and Mary. Jane's daughter Rowena lived with them also and is listed in the census as 'idiotic'. My grandfather William is shown in the 1880 Federal Census as living with Jeremy Haisington, his wife and children, in nearby Lincoln, Iowa in Mitchell County. William is listed as a laborer and was 23 years old then. Jane disappears from the Federal Census records between the 1880 and 1900 census, so she probably passed on during this period. Unfortunately, most of the 1890 federal census records were destroyed by a fire in Washington, DC thus creating a 20 year record gap in the crucial years of my families history.

Additonal Canfield records of interest show the following: In 1900, Everton Canfield with his wife Carrie and children: Harry, Charles, Nora, Ralph, Hazel, Willard and Nellie were living in Crook County, Wyoming. The 1920 Federal Census shows Everton living in Casper, Wyoming with his son-in-law Vernon Stanley, his daughter Nora, and with four children probably belonging to Vernon and Nora.

The 1930 Federal Census lists the following Canfields: Calvert Canfield, age 84, living alone in McDougald, Lake-of-the Woods County, Minnesota; and Charles Canfield, age 62, living alone in Franklin, Idaho. These men are most likely Emerson and Jane's and Everton and Carrie's sons respectively.

William G. Canfield, 1854 – 1897

Will G. Canfield was Grandma Black's first husband and is my maternal grandfather. He was a carpenter. Will, or William was born February 20, 1854 in Walworth County near Hudson, Wisconsin, and died March 18, 1897 in Todd County, Minnesota. He married Alice Belle Sarff on April 1, 1883. Will and Alice had three children: Harriet aka Ella in 1884, Elsie (my mother) in 1888, and Leo in 1892. Will's parents. Emerson and Jane or (Mary Jane) Canfield were born in Massachusetts or Connecticut and New Hampshire, respectively, and moved to Hudson in or about 1845. The family moved to Cedar Township in Floyd County, Iowa following Emerson's death. We believe that their ancestors came from England but we can't prove that.

We have found records of Dr. A. Canfield, a Long Prairie physician, and of Manning Canfield, a pharmacist in Long Prairie, but have yet to establish a linkage with Will. There is a story that when Will first laid eyes on the pretty young Alice Belle Sarff that he said, "I'm going to marry her!" And so he did.

I never had the privilege of knowing my Grandpa Canfield.

Elsie Cecil Canfield Edam, 1888 – 1939

Elsie is my mother. I know very little of her young life other than that she was born on November 11, 1888 in or near Browerville, Minnesota. She spent much of her life there or in and around Long Prairie. She and her older sister Ella, were very close and remained so until Ella's untimely death of a heart attack in 1928. Elsie only completed eight grades of formal education yet became the teacher of a one-room country school in that area. We have a picture of this lovely, slender young girl with a Gibson girl hairdo and high-necked blouse, sitting at her desk complete with a hand bell in the foreground. This picture must have been taken about the time that she met and married Dad. Elsie married Louis Thomas Edam, my dad, in Long Prairie on June 4, 1911. They lived in Long Prairie most of their lives until they moved to Park Rapids, living for a short period of time in Little Falls, Minnesota, about twenty miles east of Long Prairie while Dad attended business college. Mom and Dad had four children, Eula born in 1913, Elva who was stillborn in 1916, Wen born in 1918 and finally me in 1928 in Park Rapids. They moved to Park Rapids in 1927 or 1928 when Dad took a better job with the Great Northern Railroad.

I think that the Edam's early life in Park Rapids must have been pretty good. We had a car, I don't know what kind except that it was big and square and looked like a large box on big wheels. Wen had a pony and Eula had a piano and piano lessons. Our rented house on Washington Street had nice trees in front and a small garage or barn in back. I expect that we were considered a middle-class family at that point; but, that all changed over night with Dad's tragic death in 1930.

When I think of Mom in those later years, I regret that many of my memories of her were of an unhappy, overworked lady. We were poor, instantly, really poor. We shortly moved from Washington Street back across the tracks to the neighborhood where I was born. Mom's last nine years of life must have been unbelievably difficult. I have memories of her crying softly to herself as she did her chores around the house. The Great Depression was in full swing. Roosevelt's three-letter programs had not yet started to take effect and Mom was too proud to take advantage of what help was available from the government or from anyone else. The Gray House was hot in the summer and cold in the winter. Yet we survived. The only income that we had then was what Mom generated herself from selling eggs and chickens from a small flock and milk from our one cow.

She fed us from her garden and from our animals. Our fare was simple, yet I don't recall ever going hungry. In spite of all this, I do not think of my childhood as unhappy. Difficult, probably yes, but Mom gave me a life of freedom and independence that few other boys enjoyed.

Until Wen bought a well used Model A Ford Roadster in about 1936, we walked wherever we went. We walked across the railroad tracks and through the municipal park anytime that we went downtown to buy groceries. At that time, we walked across town to visit Grandma and the cousins. I walked to and from school every day and almost always came home for lunch. Nearly every Sunday we walked to Riverside Methodist Church for church and Sunday school. Mom had me baptized into the church when I was five or six years old. One summer she sent me to

Bible School at the Baptist Church. I didn't like this much, but I didn't argue. Those Baptists were strict and humorless and not much fun. They even had a spy in a window across from the Royal Theater to report on sinful members who attended the movies. Fun bunch.

Mom's life must have been a little easier when Eula and later Wen started working and contributed cash to the family fortune. Then in 1937 or 1938, she worked for the town as a matron at the swimming beach, where I learned to swim. That was a good summer, for me, anyway.

She was a quiet, kindly, Christian woman. Some of our neighbors were not, however. One neighbor would frequently come home drunk and would beat his wife and kids. On more than one morning, I would awake to find our small house full of sleeping neighbor kids and their mother. And, she fed the bums that rode in the boxcars on the nearby railroad and knocked at our door looking for handouts.

She was a good mother to me. I recall sitting on her lap in the living room as she rocked me and sang songs to me from a composition book that she had filled with lyrics and poems clipped from newspapers. We have recently found that composition book and will preserve it as part of her heritage.

Another fond memory is of Mom and I sitting at the kitchen table by lamplight paging through the latest Spiegel catalog picking out those items that we would buy "if we had the money". My favorite was a red bicycle that cost $19.95, a fortune for us in those days. I still measure purchases today in terms of how many red Spiegel bicycles an item in question would cost.

Mom was forgiving of most of my shortcomings but drew a firm line with others. I recall consequences from some of my unfortunate choice of words that I uttered within her hearing. She defended me when I unintentionally hit Helen Town in the head with a large stone. I recall a tearful evening when she was told of my friends and my game of doctor and subsequent exploration of each other's bodies. But she saved me from smoking when I observed her extreme unhappiness the night that she discovered that Wen had started to smoke. I vowed then and there that I would never smoke and I never did, not even corncob pipes and corn silk.

One hot summer evening in 1939, my cousin Leo and I were watching a movie at the Park Theater when Mr. Turnblad, our band director, came down the aisle and took us from the theater to the small, old hospital north on Main Street. Mom had been taken to the hospital a few days before, but it never occurred to me then that her stay would be anything but short. I didn't even know why she was there. That night when we were taken to her room, most of the family was there, quietly weeping. Mom was not conscious even though her eyes were open. I'm sure that she didn't recognize me. It was suggested that I give her a kiss and I kissed her dry, feverish, unresponsive lips. Then my cousins took me to their house where I spent the night. The next morning, I awoke to be informed that Mom had died. It was July 31, 1939.

The following days are a blur. I recall sleeping at various houses and taking meals with different people. I recall sitting in the front row of folding chairs at Frazee's Funeral Home and kissing her cold lips through a veil of gauze. Then she was gone and my life changed forever.

Ella & Elsie 1905

Grandma Black

Alice 1916

Long Prairie circa 1924

The 3 Musketeers 1926

My Cousins Long Prairie 1923

III. EDAM ANCESTRY

Louis and Sabina Eidam, 1800 – circa 1880

We believe that Louis and Sabina M. (probably Mary) Eidam are my fraternal great grandparents. We know very little of them other that we believe that they came from Virginia but were born in Germany, probably around Brunswig, and moved from Virginia before the beginning of the Civil War, probably in the 1850s. We are searchng for their parents and have found two likely candidates. The 1840 Federal Census lists Benjamin Edam living in Botecourt County in Virginia; born about 1780. The 1850 Federal Census lists Elizabeth B. Edam living in Regiment 22, Mechlenburg County, Virginia. She was born about 1795. It now appears that while they may be related to Louis and Sabina, the search for my great, great grandparents will probably have to be done in Brunswig or Prussia in Germany. The 1880 Federal Census shows Louis Eidam age 78 and Sabina M. Eidam age 80 living with a son, Fredrick, age 47, and grandchildren in Hennepin County, Minnetonka Township, Minnesota. Louis is listed as a retired cooper who was born in Prussia. His wife, Sabina M. Eidam was born in Brunswig, Germany. Also residing in Minnetonka Township in this census is Edward H. Eidam age 41 and his family. At a house not far from Fredrick resides George W. Eidam, age 36, blind and divorced. (See the George W. Edam paragraph in the section that follows. It seems very likely that they are one and the same man.)

George William Edam, 1844 – 1908

George William Edam, my fraternal grandfather, has been the most difficult to trace and has turned out to be the most colorful and interesting of all my ancestors so far. He is somewhat of a chameleon so what I report as 'facts' herein, may or may not be so.

George first shows up in marriage records when he married Mary E. French in Beetown, Wisconsin on March 9, 1867. He next appears in Prairie du Chien, Wisconsin, in the 1870 Federal Census, age 26, a cooper and blind. There is no mention of Mary French and no mention of children. Later in 1870, December 8th, George married Fanny Daniels, her second marriage and probably his as well. William and Fanny had a son , Bert Oliver Edam who became the head of the Montana Edam branch, and my father's half-brother. It is not clear if Bert was born in Minnesota or near Arena, Wisconsin.

According to Fanny, George went by the name of William or Will rather than George. He was blind in one eye from an accident working as a cooper. She said that he also worked as a traveling musician, playing fiddle and Jews harp in dancehalls and saloons around the area. We are told that at one time, he was a driver for Wells Fargo on the Fort Dearborn, Fort Crawford, Prairie du Chien route. A Chicago newspaper reported that Will Edam drove the first load of lumber into town for reconstruction of the city after the "Mrs. O'Leary's Cow" fire in October 1871 had destroyed much of the city.

'William' Edam then "just disappeared." He was reported as (a) killed by Indians; (b) killed by robbers while driving for Wells Fargo; (c) shot and killed in a barroom brawl while fiddling; or (d) none of the above. It seems that (d) is the correct answer; none of these deaths actually happened. He probably decided to start a new life and "just disappeared."

He next appeared in the 1880 Federal Census living in Hennepin County, Minnetonka Township in Minnesota. He is listed as George W. Eidam, age 36, blind, divorced and born in Virginia with parents born in Prussia and Brunswig. At that time he was living with Sylvia Meyer, age 24 and a daughter (his?) Henrietta age one. His next appearance of record was in 1885 living in a boarding house in Ellsworth Township, Meeker County, Minnesota, apparently single and unattached. He then married my fraternal grandmother, Mariah or Maria Farries Evans on November 4, 1889 in Meeker County. My dad, Louis Thomas Edam, was born to George and Mariah on October 23, 1890, we think in a log house near Clotho, Minnesota. This log house, or one nearly identical to it, can be seen today about one mile west of Clotho.

George William reportedly had four wives, maybe more. In any event, he spent the rest of his life with my Grandmother Edam and died June 5, 1908, in Leslie Township, Todd County, Minnesota where he is buried in the Cemetery of the United Brethern Church in Leslie. The following obituary is abstracted from similar reports for June, 1908 issues of the *Long Prairie Leader* and the *Long Prairie Argus:*

"Grandpa Edam, the blind gentleman who resided near Clotho, died at his home last Friday after a long illness. The funeral was held from the U. B. Church in Leslie and the internment took place in the cemetery of that church. A large crowd of his friends attended. Mr. Edam had been blind for over 40 years. Death was the result of the infirmities of old age. He was born in Virginia and had been a resident of Todd County for a long time. His wife and son have the sympathy of their neighbors."

Claudia and I have visited two cemetaries near Clotho, but have, as yet, been unable to locate his grave.

Mariah (Maria) Farries Evans Edam – 1842 - 1927

My Fraternal Grandmother is Mariah (or Maria) Farries

Evans Edam, born in Yorkshire, England in 1842; exact birthplace is unknown. She emigrated to the United States in 1846 and later married William J. Evans and gave birth to five children to go with five stepchildren that Will Evans brought to the marriage. She was widowed and then married George William Edam in Meeker County, Minnesota in November 4, 1889 and gave birth to my father, Louis Thomas Edam in 1890. They resided near Clotho in Leslie Township, Todd County for some time prior to George's death in 1908. Mariah then moved to Stillwater, Minnesota where she lived with her daughter, Minnie Evans Love until her death on September 8, 1927. She is buried in Hutchinson, Minnesota. Her grave can be found in the older part of that cemetery, next to the graves of some of her children.

Louis Thomas Edam, 1890 – 1930

I have few memories of my father. How many could there be when he died shortly after my second birthday? Yet there are certain memories that were etched permanently into my mind even back then. I clearly remember standing by the side of the gravel road in front of our house in Park Rapids waiting for him to come home from work at the depot. This is followed immediately by the memory of him coming up the street in his bib overalls and swinging me up into his arms.

I remember standing beside him outside our garage while he cleaned a large fish that he had nailed to a board. It must have been the muskie that he is holding in an old photograph that is included in this book. The picture was taken on the platform of the Great Northern Railroad depot in Park Rapids where he worked as a section hand and as a station agent.

And finally I have a freeze-frame image of his gray casket

in our living room with people standing there weeping.

I would have liked to have known him better. Eula and my cousin Alice said that he was a good man who loved his family. He must have been the *de facto* leader of the family because Grandma and my cousins followed when he moved to Park Rapids.

I know that he loved to hunt and to fish. He was very tall for those years; I believe that he stood over six feet four inches in height. He was slender if not thin and some of his friends called him 'Slim' but most everyone called him 'Louie'. His pictures show piercing eyes and a hawk nose. We have a picture of him, taken when he probably was in his early twenties, a dandy in a tight jacket with a too small bowler hat perched on his head. The picture was taken in St. Paul. I wonder what story might accompany that picture.

He attended a business college in Little Falls, Minnesota for a short time, and he worked in a general store for a while, in Long Prairie. He belonged to the Home Guard of Minnesota in Long Prairie and was scheduled to go to France with his rifle company when the World War I ended in 1918. He smoked a pipe and played the violin, the same violin that I believe belonged to his father. Mom let me play with the violin when we lived in the Gray House.

I believe that Dad was born, and spent his youth, near Clotho, Minnesota in Leslie Township. Long Prairie newspapers in 1908 report that he pitched for the Clotho ball team, went to North Dakota for the wheat harvest and apparently was somewhat of a ladies man. In 1910, the Federal Census found Dad living with his step-sister in Long Prairie. Next door were the Canfields! This no doubt is how Dad and Mom met. We do know his father's name, George William Edam or Eidam, and that George was born in Virginia but we don't know exactly where.

Dad married Elsie Canfield, a rural school teacher, on June 4, 1911 in Long Prairie. We have the original marriage certificate. He was a good father to Eula, to Wen and to me.

His life came to an early conclusion on October 26, 1930 while he was duck hunting on Moran Lake south of Park Rapids. The story as I know it is that Dad had shot some ducks from the lakeshore with the ducks falling onto the ice at the edge of the lake. He had borrowed a boat that was pulled up on the shore and had set out to retrieve them. Shortly thereafter, the boat capsized throwing Dad into the water. He clung to the overturned boat for a time. Mr. Moran, who may have witnessed the accident or heard his cries for help shouted to him to hold on while he went for help. When help returned, Dad was gone. He died alone in the frigid water.

Years later, while waiting to leave for the Navy, I bicycled to Moran Lake, borrowed a boat, rowed around the lake, caught some fish and swam naked, wondering if I was close to the spot where he drowned. I still wonder.

His grave and headstone can be found along side Mom's in Evergreen Cemetery outside of Browerville, Minnesota.

Eula Lorrain Edam Jensen, 1913 – 2000

Since I have spent more time over the years with my sister Eula than with Wen or with either of my parents, I should know more about her than I do. I know that she was born in Long Prairie, Minnesota on January 8, 1913 and lived there until the family moved to Park Rapids in the late 1920s. I know that during the Long Prairie years, she was very close to her female cousins, especially with Leola Canfield Zastrow and with Alice Gadbaw Nichols. These friendships continued until Alice's death and until Eula's passing in 2000.

Eula was a shadow figure in my life until Mom's death in 1939. Then she was thrust, with Wen, into the role of my caretaker until I graduated from high school and left for the Navy. After Eula graduated from high school she attended a year of Normal Training. This was a local preparatory course for rural teachers. Following completion of this course, she taught, for only a year, I believe, all eight grades at a one-room country school near Hubbard, Minnesota, boarding with a farm family near the school. I vaguely remember that this was not a happy time for Eula. After her teaching experience, she took a job as a clerk at the Hubbard County Courthouse for the princely salary of $90 per month. Those was big bucks in those days! Later she worked as a clerk at the Ben Franklin Store and still later for Minnesota Power and Light Company. She worked for a time as a pattern cutter for Singer Manufacturing when they set up shop in the American Legion Building in the late '40s. She even tried her hand at selling advertising for a Lutheran Brotherhood publication traveling throughout southern Minnesota and Iowa. But that was not her cup of tea either. She bought a car and learned to drive in the mid '50s and soon earned a reputation, probably deserved, as a 'leadfoot'. She picked up a few speeding tickets and became acquainted with one or two troopers with the Minnesota State Highway Patrol.

I recall that she carried the torch for one of the amateur boxers who boarded with us for a short time when we all lived at the Gray House. Other than that, I doubt if she had many if any romantic encounters.

Other than the fact that she had the warmest room in the house, I have very few memories of Eula in those years. On one occasion, Mom cautioned me to be nice to Eula because she was 'nervous'. I never understood what that meant. Like Wen, Eula was very quiet, a private person.

But unlike Wen, it was easy to tell when Eula was upset about something. She had a glare that was legendary when she lived with us in Colorado.

She sang in the Methodist Church choir but had few other activities outside the church that I can remember. She belonged to the Lady Lions in Buffalo, Minnesota and to the Homemakers and the Young at Hearts in Monument, Colorado.

After Mom died, and following an unworkable attempt for we three remaining Edams to live with Grandma Black and the five cousins in their small house, we moved into an apartment, actually half of Dutton's house, near the Gray House. After Wen married Bonnie Jeanne, Eula and I moved into a small apartment above the Gamble Store on Main Street and finally to one across the street above the Ben Franklin Store. These had to be difficult years for Eula. We had very little money and few prospects for improving our life style. In addition, she had a teenage boy, me, on her hands. Not a pretty picture.

Eula moved to the Twin Cities in the 1950s, lived with us for a short time and then answered an ad in the Tribune to be a live-in baby sitter and house keeper for a family in northeast Minneapolis. One job followed another. This time, she married her employer, Alton Christian Jensen, on September 25, 1969, his fourth wife. Following Al's retirement from his beer bar and restaurant business on Lake Street, they bought a small house in Buffalo, Minnesota where they lived until his death in 1985.

Eula came to Colorado in 1988 and lived with Claudia and me until 1995 when she moved to a retirement apartment in Edina, Minnesota. She lived out her remaining years in Edina until her death from cancer on April 12, 2000. Her remains were cremated and her ashes scattered in the same cemetery in northeast Minneapolis where her husband is buried. I have always felt that she sacrificed her life for me. I have tried to repay her, if such is possible, but feel that I came up short. I wish that she could have had a happier life.

Elva Edam, 1916

Elva Edam, my sister, was stillborn in 1916. Her grave is near those of my parents outside of Browerville, Minnesota.

Wendell Ray Edam 1918 – 1990

My brother Wen was born in Long Prairie, Minnesota on August 31, 1918. I know very little about his boyhood in Long Prairie except that he and his two cousins, Ken and Bill Gadbaw were very close and played together a lot. They called themselves "The Three Musketeers".

Wen and I were born ten years apart, and because of this age difference, we were not all that close. Never the less, we interacted enough that I have quite a few good memories of him. I'll relate some of these memories here and you'll find more in 'the book'. Some of these memories are a little bizarre, but I have at least one picture to offer as proof positive of the event.

Wen was an outdoors person; he loved to fish and to hunt. He had a passion for these sports as long as I knew him. Probably my first recollection of Wen was when he nailed me to the garage. It wasn't quite as bad as it first sounds. Wen had gone fishing and caught a nice stringer of fish, six or eight of them. Being rightly proud of his accomplishment, he wanted a picture of himself with his catch. He needed someone to hold the other end of the stringer and selected me. I wanted nothing to do with this whole affair. So, he nailed one end of the stringer to the garage wall and nailed me there also so that it looked like I was holding it. The nails went through my clothes into the wall so I wasn't hurt; but I wasn't very happy about it either. The picture in another part of this document is proof of this episode. Do I look happy in the photo? I don't think so.

In later years, Wen held the state record for Brown Trout with a seven-pound six-ounce beauty that he caught in Straight River. Ironically, a fisherman from St. Paul caught one a few ounces larger a few weeks later, also from Straight River. I wonder if the larger fish might have been fed a lead sinker diet at weigh in. Shame on me for this thought.

Wen had a black Shetland pony named Tony. One day when Mom and Dad had gone somewhere, leaving me in the care of Eula and my cousins, Wen led Tony into and through the house scaring the daylights out of the girls. I don't know if the girls ever told Mom and Dad what happened, but I vaguely remember the incident and heard the story repeated over the years.

My memories of Wen have a gap of a few years that lasted until he was in high school. He played basketball for the Park Rapids Panthers and was on the High School Stock Judging Team. The team traveled around northwestern Minnesota with their coach and competed with other teams in judging quality of cattle. I don't believe that Park Rapids has had such a team for many years.

He played trumpet in the high school and municipal bands as well in a six-piece orchestra called the Night Owls. They played in nightclubs (a very euphemistic term) around Park Rapids playing in such sophisticated venues as Wolf Lake, Sebeka, Menahga and other towns within a reasonable drive of Park Rapids. They even once broadcast a brief show over WDAY in Fargo. The members of the Night Owls wore black trousers and white tuxedo jackets with bow ties and sat behind black and white 'fronts' made of plywood. These 'fronts' served as music holders in addition to giving them a big band image. They sometimes practiced in our living room, always an event for me. I thought they were great; Wen and Dean Hedlund were on trumpets, Orv Reynolds on piano, Gene Meyers on drums, and I think Solon Green played trombone. I can't remember who played saxophone. I will always remember *Margie, Darktown Strutter's Ball, My Blue Heaven* and other songs from that era that were part of their repertoire. Wen's share of the band's profits brought a few badly needed dollars into the family coffers.

Wen was also a singer. He had a soft, almost shy tenor voice. He frequently sang solos in church as well as at funerals in addition to the church choir.

He bought his first car while he was in high school, a Model A Ford convertible complete with rumble seat. It was a neat little car and especially fun to ride in the rumble seat. Wen sometimes took us on a Sunday drive generally on country roads around PR and sometimes as far as Itasca State Park. It was a rare outing when we didn't have to stop and repair a flat tire.

Besides helping Mom care for the livestock, Wen had a part time job sweeping out the old post office. He sometimes pressed me into service giving me the delightful job of emptying the cuspidors or spitoons as they were also called. To this day, the odor of sweeping compound nearly causes me to barf and I don't even want to think about spitoons.

He worked for awhile at Green's Grocery on Main Street, full time after he graduated from high school in 1936. Coincidentally, and years later, when Wen opened Edam's Shoe Store, it was in the same building that Green's Grocery had occupied. In between those times, Wen worked for Bishop's Clothing Store at the other end of block where he managed the shoe department for many years. He stayed there until he and Bonnie opened Edam's Shoe Store in 1970 or thereabouts.

Wen must have had a number of girl friends, he was a pretty good looking guy, but I don't recall any until he started to date Bonnie Jeanne Swaim. Bonnie Jeanne was beautiful. They were married and lived happily ever after. Really! They have two daughters, my nieces, Judy Edam Ham and Jane Edam Schmitz. Jane and Tom live in Detroit Lakes, Minnesota and have four children: Brenda, Brian, Stacy and Stephanie. Judy and Dale live in Terrel, Texas and have two daughters: Sharien and Karien. Wen failed his draft physical for WWII because of an undersized heart consequently he was given to fainting spells when he encountered blood or the prospect of blood. Two occasions come to mind that involve this physical quirk. One nice fall day, Wen had taken Bonnie Jeanne with him while he hunted partridge. Bonnie got tired of walking so she sat down to wait for Wen as he hunted around a small hill. Wen cautioned her not to move around while he was gone. Ignoring Wen's warning, Bonnie Jeanne got up and wandered around the hill. About this time, Wen flushed a bird and shot at it not knowing that Bonnie was near his line of fire. One nearly spent pellet from Wen's shotgun struck his wife just above the eye. The wound was not serious, but it was bleeding quite a bit. As they walked back to the car, Wen would faint every so often, so Bonnie Jeanne had to stop and revive him as he escorted her to medical assistance.

Years later, however, in 1947, on Wen's first and only attempt at deer hunting, the opposite situation occurred. Wen had just shot a doe, and he and Frank Sullivan, his hunting partner, were preparing to hang the deer up in order to dress it out. At that moment, another hunter who had been tracking the doe came out of the woods and began shooting. Both Wen and Frank were wearing red and were clearly visible. One of the bullets went through Frank's knee and lodged in Wen's shinbone. On this occasion, Wen helped his seriously injured friend out of the woods with a bullet lodged in his own leg. No fainting this time. Frank later lost his leg. The local, experienced, hunter who did the shooting never came to the hospital nor ever apologized to either Wen or Frank. Go figure.

Wen was a quiet man, who rarely lost his temper, although I can remember one such occasion. It was a cold winter day and when Wen was trying to start his car with a hand crank. This was not only a difficult and tedious job, it was dangerous. There were many broken arms in those days when the 'crankers' hand would slip off the crank handle and then was struck in the forearm by backlash from the compression powered crank handle. The fracture was always about eight inches above the wrist. Anyway, Wen had been cranking away for some time without success and finally ran out of patience. I was playing in the snow outside the garage when suddenly the crank came flying out of the garage door followed closely by a string of invective, composed of words, many of which I had not yet learned. This was not typical of Wen, ever.

Wen died February 17, 1990 in Detroit Lakes, Minnesota of emphysema and subsequent heart failure. His grave is located in Oak Grove Cemetery in Detroit Lakes along side that of his wife, Bonnie Jeanne who joined him in Heaven on August 4, 2003.

And finally..........

This is all that I know of our ancestors and of my family at this time. We will continue to search for additional information and will try to pass it on to you when appropriate.

And now, the day is fast approaching when I must join my family, my ancestors and my friends in the greatest of all adventures that we all share called Death. It is my wish that my remains be reduced to ashes and that these ashes be released at some quiet and peaceful place of Claudia's choosing. When you, my readers, have occasion to pass by my final resting place, I hope that you will think of me, and I ask that you.........

"...grieve not, nor speak of me with tears, but laugh and talk of me as if I were with you...I loved you so...'twas Heaven here with you..."

Anonymous

"Blessings on your eyes and on your children. Blessings on the ground beneath you. Wherever you walk, I go with you.........Selah".

Anita Diamant from the Red Tent

The Edam Homestead circa 1889

Mariah & George Edam

Mom at her school 1910

Mom with her classes 1910

Dad about 1910 – taken in St Paul

Dad about 1910 – taken in St Paul

Louis & Elsie Edam 1911

Dad Long Prairie National Guard 1918

Dad wearing coat I slept in on cold nights – 1920

Dad with Fish

Wen & Eula 1919

Mom, Wen, Dad & Eula 1923

Eula 1916

Eula Lorrain Edam

Wendell 1919

Jane, Bonnie Jeanne, Judy, & Wen 1949

Wen nailed me to the Wall 1931

Wen & Tony 1931

Wen & Me 1940

Wen 1926

PRHS Judging Team 1936

Printed in the United States
95127LV00002B/178-189/A

9 781432 712938